Averil Macdonald

REVISION PLUS

OCR Gateway
GCSE Physics B
Revision and Classroom Companion

Contents

Scientists carry out **investigations** and collect **evidence** in order to explain how and why things happen. Scientific knowledge and understanding can lead to the **development of new technologies** that have a huge impact on **society** and the **environment**.

Scientific evidence is often based on data collected through **observations** and **measurements**. To allow scientists to reach conclusions, evidence must be **repeatable**, **reproducible** and **valid**.

Models

Models are used to explain scientific ideas and the Universe around us. Models can be used to describe:

- a complex idea – like how heat moves through a metal
- a system – like the Earth's structure.

Models make systems or ideas easier to understand by including only the most important parts. They can be used to explain real-world observations or to make predictions. But, because models don't contain all the **variables**, they sometimes make incorrect predictions.

Models and scientific ideas may change as new observations are made and new **data** are collected. Data and observations may be collected from a series of experiments. For example, the accepted model of the structure of the atom has been modified as new evidence has been collected from many experiments.

Hypotheses

Scientific explanations are called **hypotheses** – these are used to explain observations. A hypothesis can be tested by planning experiments and collecting data and evidence. For example, if you pull a metal wire you may observe that it stretches. This can be explained by the scientific idea that the atoms in the metal are arranged in layers that can slide over each other. A hypothesis can be modified as new data is collected, and may even be disproved.

Data

Data can be displayed in **tables**, **pie charts** or **line graphs**. In your exam you may be asked to:

- choose the most appropriate method for displaying data
- identify trends
- use data mathematically – including using statistical methods, calculating the mean and calculating gradients of graphs.

A Table

% Yield	Temperature			
Pressure	250°C	350°C	450°C	550°C
200 atm	73%	50%	28%	13%
400 atm	77%	65%	45%	26%

A Pie Chart

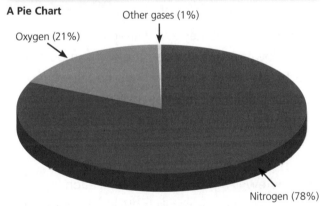

Other gases (1%)

Oxygen (21%)

Nitrogen (78%)

A Line Graph

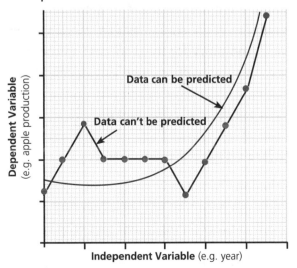

Data can be predicted

Data can't be predicted

Dependent Variable (e.g. apple production)

Independent Variable (e.g. year)

Data (cont)

Sometimes the same data can lead to different conclusions. For example, data shows that the world's average temperatures have been rising significantly over the last 200 years. Some scientists think this is due to increased combustion of fossil fuels, while other scientists think it's a natural change that has happened before during Earth's history.

Scientific and Technological Development

Every scientific or technological development can have effects that we do not know about. This can give rise to **issues**. An issue is an important question that is in dispute and needs to be settled. Issues can be:

- **social** – they impact on the human population of a community, city, country or the world
- **environmental** – they impact on the planet, its natural ecosystems and resources
- **economic** – money and related factors such as employment and the distribution of resources
- **ethical** – what is right and wrong morally; a value judgement must be made
- **cultural** – giving an insight into differences between people on local and global scales.

Peer review is a process of self-regulation involving experts in a particular field who **critically examine** the work undertaken. Peer review methods are designed to maintain standards and provide **credibility** for the work that has been carried out. The methods used vary depending on the nature of the work and also on the overall purpose behind the review process.

Evaluating Information

Conclusions can then be made based on the scientific evidence that has been collected – they should try to explain the results and observations.

Evaluations look at the whole investigation. It is important to be able to evaluate information relating to social–scientific issues. **When evaluating information**:

- make a list of **pluses** (pros)
- make a list of **minuses** (cons)
- consider how each point might **impact on society**.

You also need to consider if the source of information is reliable and credible and to consider opinions, bias and weight of evidence.

Opinions are personal viewpoints – those backed up by valid and reliable evidence carry far more weight than those based on non-scientific ideas. Opinions of experts can also carry more weight than those of non-experts. Information is **biased** if it favours one particular viewpoint without providing a balanced account. Biased information might include incomplete evidence or it might try to influence how you interpret the evidence.

Examples of these processes are included in the main content of this book. However, it is important to remember that fundamental scientific processes are relevant to all areas of science.

P1: Energy for the Home

This module looks at:

- How heat and temperature are different, and the use of water to heat homes.
- Insulation, energy efficiency and energy transfer through conduction, convection and radiation.
- Electromagnetic waves and their uses.
- Light and its uses in digital communication.
- Radiations in the electromagnetic spectrum and the properties, dangers and uses of infrared and microwave radiation.
- Infrared radiation and its uses in the home and in transmitting signals.
- Global communication and the benefits, uses and impacts on society of wireless transmission.
- Waves, how they carry information and how they can be harmful to organisms, as well as how climate is affected by natural and human activity.

Heat Flow

Every year we spend millions of pounds heating our houses but much of this heat energy escapes through our windows and roofs. We can use our understanding of temperature and heat flow to help us to reduce our energy usage and save us money.

Temperature

Temperature is a measure of how hot something is. The unit of measurement is **degrees Celsius, °C**. **Heat** is a form of **energy** and is measured in **joules, J**.

> **Temperature** is a measurement of how **hot** something is using a chosen scale, usually degrees Celsius, °C, but sometimes degrees Fahrenheit, °F.
>
> Heat is a measurement of **energy** on an **absolute scale** – always in **joules, J**.

If there is a difference in temperature between an object and its surroundings then this results in the flow of heat energy from the **hotter** region to the **cooler** region, making the hotter region cool down and the cooler region warm up. A hot region is the **source**; the cold region is the **sink**.

If an object's **temperature rises** it is **taking in heat energy**. For example, if you take a can of cola out of the fridge it will soon warm up to room temperature because the can and the liquid take in heat energy from the air in the room.

If an object's **temperature falls** it is **giving out heat energy**. For example, a hot cup of tea will soon cool down, eventually reaching room temperature. If you hold it in your hands you will feel the heat energy flowing from the cup into your hands.

When an object has a **very high temperature** compared to its surroundings it will **cool down very quickly**. As its temperature gets nearer room temperature, it will cool down at a slower rate.

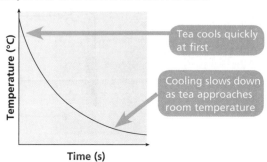

Tea cools quickly at first

Cooling slows down as tea approaches room temperature

> The molecules in all solid materials are vibrating, so they have **kinetic energy**. The higher the temperature of an object, the higher the average kinetic energy of the molecules.

Thermograms

Temperature can be represented by a range of colours in a **thermogram**.

- The windows are where most heat energy is escaping so they show up as white (hottest), yellow or red.
- The well-insulated loft is where the least heat energy is escaping so this shows up as black (coldest), dark blue or purple.

Measuring Heat Energy

The amount of energy needed to raise the temperature of an object depends on:

- the **mass** of the object
- the **change in temperature** required
- the **specific heat capacity** (see opposite) of the material that the object is made of.

This experiment measures the amount of heat energy needed to change the temperature of an aluminium block.

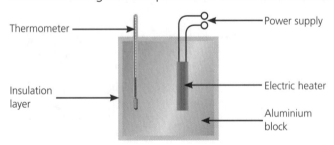

Thermometer

Power supply

Insulation layer

Electric heater

Aluminium block

The electric heater provides 100J of heat energy per second. Therefore, if you time how many seconds it takes for the temperature of the aluminium to rise by a certain amount, e.g. 10°C, you can calculate the total amount of energy used to make the temperature rise using the following formula:

Total energy supplied	=	Energy supplied per second	×	Number of seconds

It takes 50 seconds to raise the temperature of the aluminium block by 10°C.

So, 100J/s × 50s

= 5000J ← The total energy supplied

Specific Heat Capacity

The **specific heat capacity of a material** is the energy needed to raise the temperature of **1kg** of the material by **1°C**.

Each material has its own value, which measures how much energy it needs to raise its temperature by 1°C. For example, it takes more energy to raise the temperature of a liquid by 1°C than to raise the temperature of a solid by 1°C (liquids have higher specific heat capacities than solids).

The following equation is used to find the amount of energy required to raise the temperature of an object by a certain amount:

Energy (J)	=	Mass (kg)	×	Specific heat capacity (J/kg/°C)	×	Temperature change (°C)

Example 1

The specific heat capacity of copper is 387J/kg/°C. Calculate how much heat energy is required to raise the temperature of a 5kg block of copper by 10°C. Use the formula:

$$\text{Energy} = \text{Mass} \times \frac{\text{Specific heat}}{\text{capacity}} \times \frac{\text{Temperature}}{\text{change}}$$

$$= 5\text{kg} \times 387\text{J/kg/°C} \times 10\text{°C} = \mathbf{19\,350J}$$

Example 2

It takes 28 800J of heat energy to raise the temperature of a 4kg block of aluminium from 22°C to 30°C. Calculate the specific heat capacity of aluminium. Rearrange the formula:

$$\text{Specific heat capacity} = \frac{\text{Energy}}{\text{Mass} \times \text{Temperature change}}$$

$$= \frac{28\,800J}{4\text{kg} \times 8\text{°C}} = \mathbf{900J/kg/°C}$$

Melting and Boiling

The data below shows how the temperature of some water in a kettle changed over 300 seconds.

Time (s)	0	30	60	90	120	150
Temperature (°C)	21	39	55	68	79	88
Time (s) (cont)	180	210	240	270	300	
Temperature (°C)	95	100	100	100	100	

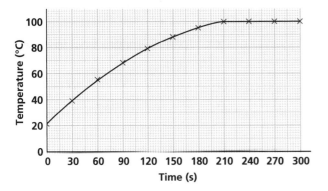

The temperature rises quickly to begin with, but once it gets to 100°C it stops rising – it remains **constant**. The temperature of the water will never rise above **100°C**, no matter how long it is heated for. This is because when the water reaches 100°C, all the **heat energy** supplied by the kettle is being used to **boil** the water instead of heating it up.

Likewise, when you put an **ice cube** in a drink it does not **melt** immediately because it needs **energy** to warm it to 0°C, and then more energy to make it melt – its temperature stays at 0°C while it melts.

The temperature of a material does not change when it is **boiling**, **melting** or **freezing** (i.e. changing state). So, to **interpret data** showing the heating or cooling of an object, look for places where the temperature stays the same.

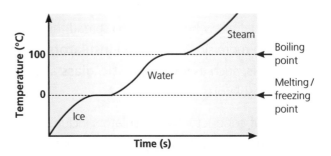

During the melting and boiling of water, the energy supplied is used to break **intermolecular bonds** (instead of raising its temperature) as the water changes state from solid to liquid and from liquid to gas. This explains why the temperature of the material does not change – none of the energy is being used to heat up the material. All the energy is being used to break bonds.

Specific Latent Heat

The amount of heat energy required to melt or boil 1kg of a material is called its **specific latent heat**. It depends on:

- the **material**
- the **state** (solid, liquid or gas).

The energy required to boil or melt a certain mass of a material can be found using the equation:

> **Energy** (J) **=** **Mass** (kg) **✗** **Specific latent heat** (J/kg)

Example
The specific latent heat of ice is 330 000J/kg. An ice sculpture at 0°C with a mass of 10kg is left to melt. Calculate the amount of energy required to melt the ice. Use the equation:

Energy = Mass × Specific latent heat
= 10kg × 330 000J/kg
= **3 300 000J**

Explaining Heat Transfer

Conduction and Insulation

Materials that allow heat energy to spread through them quickly are called **conductors**. **Metals** are good conductors of heat.

Materials that allow heat energy to spread through them much more slowly are called **insulators**. Most **non-metals,** such as **wood**, **plastic**, **glass** and **air,** are good insulators.

Examples of conductors and insulators include:

- A saucepan is made of a good conductor to get the heat to the food, e.g. copper or aluminium.
- A saucepan handle is made of a good insulator to stop the heat getting to your hand, e.g. wood or plastic.
- Clothing and bedding are both good insulators, because they trap air within their material, and between the layers to stop heat leaving your body.
- Curtains are good insulators because they trap a layer of air between them and the window, which helps to reduce heat energy loss by conduction.

Convection Currents

When air next to a radiator in a room gets warm it will expand and become less dense, so it will rise up and cooler air will move in to take its place. So hot air rises and warms up the air already at ceiling level. This movement of air is called a **convection current**.

Circulation of Air Caused by a Radiator

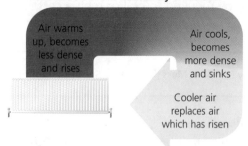

Air warms up, becomes less dense and rises

Air cools, becomes more dense and sinks

Cooler air replaces air which has risen

Reflecting Infrared

Heat can also move as **infrared radiation** (a type of electromagnetic wave). Infrared can be reflected from shiny surfaces but is very easily absorbed by dark or rough surfaces. This is why putting a shiny surface behind a hot object will reflect the heat, but a dark surface will get very hot.

Why Are Things Hot?

If an object is heated, its particles will start to move more quickly – so a hotter object has faster moving particles. In a solid the particles move by vibrating. In a liquid and a gas the particles move around, flowing past each other and moving further apart – which is why hot air is less dense and rises.

Some examples of heat transfer are listed below:

- A hot-water tank is made of stainless steel, which reduces heat loss by radiation.
- Hot water tanks usually have an insulating jacket made of foam to reduce heat loss by conduction and convection.
- Refrigerators are insulated to reduce heat gain by conduction and convection.

Reducing Heat Losses in the Home

Apart from curtains, there are many ways to reduce heat loss from a home. It is important to think about the **payback time** – how long it takes to pay for the **insulation** from the savings you make. The diagram shows how heat can escape from a house, and the methods that can reduce heat loss.

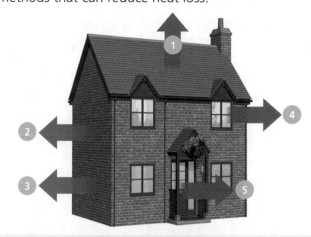

Insulation Method	Cost	Annual Saving	Payback Time
1 Fibreglass loft insulation	£400	£80	5 years
2 Reflective foil on walls behind radiators	£40	£10	4 years
3 Cavity wall insulation	£600	£30	20 years
4 Double glazing	£1800	£60	30 years
5 Draught excluders	£40	£40	1 year

Saving Energy in the Home

Houses lose energy through doors, windows, floors, walls and roofs. Energy is lost from a **source** to a **sink**, so when heat is lost from the home, the home is the source and the atmosphere is the sink. Each design feature in the house on the previous page helps to save energy by reducing heat loss. The table below explains how.

Method of Insulation	Reduces...	How?
Fibreglass loft insulation	• Conduction • Convection	• By trapping layers of air (a good insulator) between the fibres.
Reflective foil on walls behind radiators	• Radiation	• By reflecting infrared heat energy into the room.
Cavity wall insulation	• Conduction • Convection	• By trapping air (a good insulator) in the foam.
Double glazing	• Conduction • Convection	• By trapping air (a good insulator) between the panes of glass.
Draught excluders	• Convection	• By keeping as much warm air inside as possible.

(HT) Each method of house insulation helps to save energy by conduction, convection and radiation.

Other energy-saving strategies include drawing curtains early in the evening to reduce heat loss by convection, having carpets and sealed floors to stop heat loss through the floor and keeping inside doors to conservatories closed in cold weather.

Energy Efficiency

Energy efficiency is a measure of how good an appliance is at converting **input energy** (the energy supplied) into **useful output energy**.

For a television, the input energy is electrical energy and the useful energy output is light and sound. We need to be able to see and hear the programmes. But televisions also produce heat energy which, in this case, is wasted energy.

This equation is used to calculate energy efficiency:

$$\text{Efficiency \%} = \frac{\text{Useful output energy (J)}}{\text{Total energy input (J)}} \times 100\%$$

Example

An old style 60 watt light bulb uses 60 joules of electrical energy every second. In 50 seconds it gives out 300 joules of light energy (useful energy). Use the formula to calculate the efficiency of the light bulb:

$$\text{Efficiency} = \frac{\text{Useful output energy}}{\text{Total energy input}} \times 100\%$$

$$= \frac{300}{60 \times 50} \times 100\%$$

$$= 0.1 \times 100\% = \mathbf{10\%}$$

Sankey diagrams show how much energy is transferred and where it is lost. The Sankey diagram below shows the energy delivered to customers from a power station. By working out the energy used and the energy lost at each stage the actual values can be added to the diagram to show the efficiency.

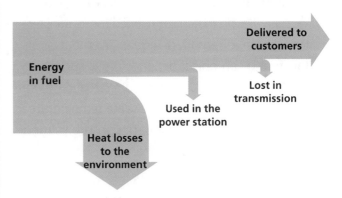

Energy in fuel → Delivered to customers / Lost in transmission / Used in the power station / Heat losses to the environment

Conduction

Conduction is the transfer of heat energy through a substance from a hotter region to a cooler region without any movement of the substance itself. As a substance, (e.g. a metal poker for a fire) is heated, the kinetic energy of its particles increases (they vibrate more). This kinetic energy is transferred between the particles in the poker and, gradually, energy is transferred along it.

Heat energy is also transferred by the free electrons in a metal. The free electrons flow, collide with and transfer energy to other atoms, increasing their kinetic energy and so the temperature rises. This is why metals are good conductors.

Insulation only stops heat loss by conduction. Heat energy can still be lost from a hot object by **radiation** and/or by **convection**. A cavity wall in a house should be filled with foam to trap air and to prevent heat loss by convection and conduction.

Convection

Because fluids (liquids) and gases can flow, they can transfer heat energy from hotter to cooler regions by their own movement. As the liquid or gas gets hotter, its particles move faster causing it to expand and become less dense. It will then rise up and be replaced by colder, denser liquid or gas.

Radiation

Radiation is the transfer of heat energy by **electromagnetic waves**. Hot objects emit mainly infrared radiation, which can pass through a vacuum, i.e. no material is needed for its transfer. How much infrared radiation is given out or taken in by an object depends on its surface:

- Dark matt surfaces emit more radiation than pale shiny surfaces at the same temperature.
- Dark matt surfaces are better absorbers (poorer reflectors) of radiation than pale shiny surfaces at the same temperature.

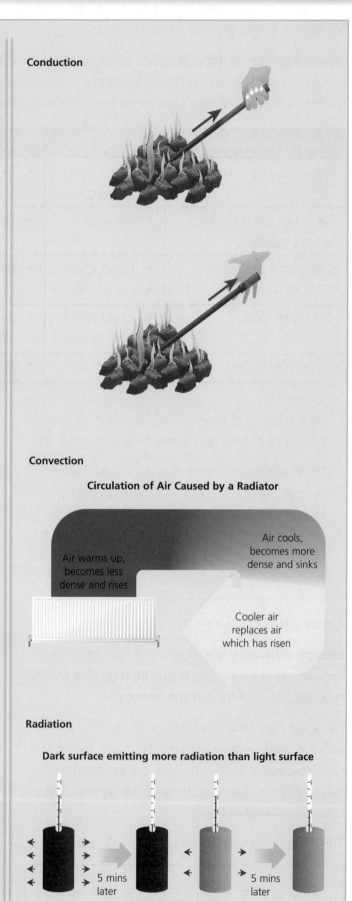

Conduction

Convection

Circulation of Air Caused by a Radiator

Air warms up, becomes less dense and rises

Air cools, becomes more dense and sinks

Cooler air replaces air which has risen

Radiation

Dark surface emitting more radiation than light surface

5 mins later

5 mins later

Transverse Waves

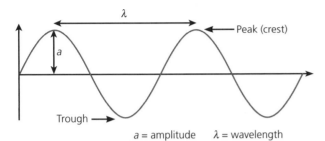

a = amplitude   λ = wavelength

All **transverse waves** have the same features:

- **Amplitude** is the maximum disturbance caused by the wave at a trough or crest (peak).
- **Wavelength** is the distance between corresponding points on two successive disturbances (i.e. from one peak to the next peak).
- **Frequency** is the number of waves produced (or that pass a particular point) in one second.

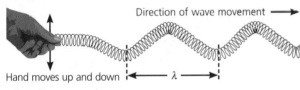

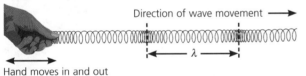

The following formula shows the relationship between wave speed, frequency and wavelength:

Wave speed (m/s) **=** **Frequency** (Hz) **×** **Wavelength** (m)

where v is wave speed, f is frequency and $λ$ is wavelength.

Example 1

Calculate the speed of this wave if its frequency is 5Hz.

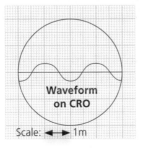

Waveform on CRO

Scale: ◄───► 1m

Wave speed = Frequency   × Wavelength

= 5Hz   × 2m

= **10m/s**

Example 2

Radio 5 Live transmits on a frequency of 909kHz. If the speed of radio waves is 300 000 000m/s, on what wavelength does it transmit? Rearrange the formula:

$$\text{Wavelength} = \frac{\text{Wave speed}}{\text{Frequency}} = \frac{300\,000\,000\text{m/s}}{909\,000\text{Hz}}$$

$$= \textbf{330m}$$

Example 3

A radio station transmits on a wavelength of 1500m. What is the frequency of the transmission?

$$\text{Frequency} = \frac{\text{Wave speed}}{\text{Wavelength}}$$

$$= \frac{3 \times 10^8}{1.5 \times 10^3} = \textbf{2 × 10}^5\textbf{Hz}$$

Reflection

Usually, when a ray of light hits a shiny surface it is **reflected**:

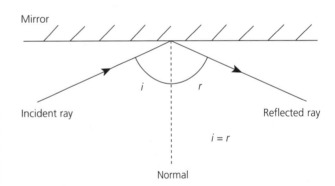

$i = r$

Multiple Reflections

Light can reflect off a series of surfaces, just like a ball bouncing off the walls in a squash court.

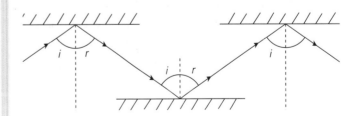

Refraction

Usually, when a ray of light or infrared passes from one material into another it changes direction – it is **refracted**. This happens because the wave changes speed:

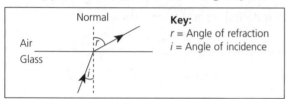

Diffraction

Diffraction is when a wave spreads out because it has passed through a narrow opening about the size of the wavelength of the wave.

Diffraction can also happen if the wave passes an obstacle. If the obstacle is large then the wavelength has to be large, otherwise there is no effect.

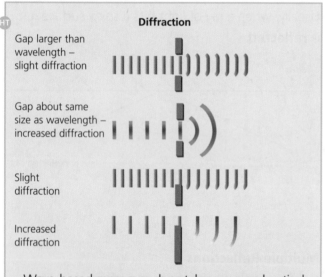

Wave-based sensors such as telescopes and optical microscopes are affected by diffraction because diffraction will limit the smallest thing they can detect. For example, two stars close together will be seen as one single star because diffraction will make the light from the two stars spread and overlap.

The Electromagnetic Spectrum

Light is one part of the **electromagnetic spectrum**. Together with the other forms of electromagnetic radiation, it makes a continuous spectrum that extends beyond each end of the **visible spectrum** (light).

Each type of electromagnetic radiation is a transverse wave that:
- travels in straight lines
- has the same speed through space (a vacuum) – 300 000 000m/s
- has a different wavelength and a different frequency.

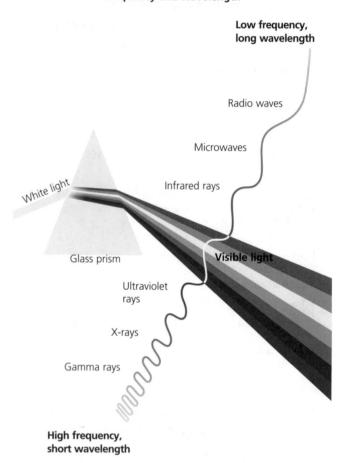

The Seven Types of Electromagnetic Waves in Order of Frequency and Wavelength

When we use electromagnetic waves for communication, the size of the receiver has to be similar to the size of the wavelength. So, satellite dishes have small receivers at their centre to detect microwaves, while television aerials are much bigger in order to detect radio waves.

Radio waves are used for TV and radio stations. Microwaves are used to communicate using satellites. Infrared and light waves are used to communicate using optical fibres.

Communicating Through Signals

Communicating through electromagnetic waves (including light) is far faster than any other means. **Morse code** was an early communication system. This is a series of 'on-off' signals with each letter of the alphabet being made up of a different pattern of dots and dashes.

Morse code was an early form of **digital** communication – digital means a code made up of a pattern of two types of input e.g. 'ons and offs'.

Signals were relayed between stations to increase the distance a message could be sent.

Now we use digital codes to transmit information along **optical fibres** as pulses of light or infrared. Using different colours (wavelengths) of light, it is possible to send many different messages along a fibre at the same time.

Communicating with Light

Like all **electromagnetic waves**, light travels very fast. The reason why modern communication is so fast is because it uses light as a signal, but the signal needs to be sent as a digital code – flashes of light.

An **optical fibre** is a long, flexible, transparent glass or plastic fibre of very small diameter. Light can travel the length of the fibre by reflecting off the sides (total internal reflection). This transfer of light depends on the **critical angle** of the substance.

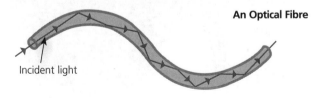

An Optical Fibre

Incident light

Critical Angle

Different media have different critical angles. The critical angle is the maximum angle (measured from the normal) at which light can be refracted and escape from a material.

At angles larger than the critical angle, the light is totally reflected back into the material. The critical angle depends on the refractive index of the medium. A large refractive index gives a smaller critical angle.

Total Internal Reflection

When the angle of incidence is bigger than the **critical angle**, the light or infrared is **totally internally reflected** and not refracted.

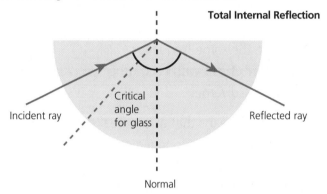

Total Internal Reflection

Incident ray

Critical angle for glass

Reflected ray

Normal

Total internal reflection can only happen inside a material that is more optically dense than the material surrounding it, such as inside glass surrounded by air, or inside Perspex surrounded by air.

Total internal reflection can also happen to light in water when the light approaches the surface and is reflected back into the water instead of emerging into the air. In all these cases the **angle of incidence** of the light has to be bigger than the **critical angle** for total internal reflection to happen. If the angle is too small some light will be refracted and escape into the air.

Comparing Communication Signals

Light, radio and electrical signals can be used for communication – they each have advantages and disadvantages:

- Light is fast but sometimes requires optical fibres.
- Radio waves can travel further, via satellites if necessary, but the signal can be lost.
- Electrical signals are reliable and can be boosted if they get weak, but they require wires.

Lasers

Lasers form very narrow beams of light of a single colour (single wavelength). They have many uses including medical (cutting skin during surgery or during dental treatment which means the patient bleeds less), cutting materials in industry, guiding weapons by reflecting off the target to show that the aim is correct, or in laser light shows.

A Medical Laser

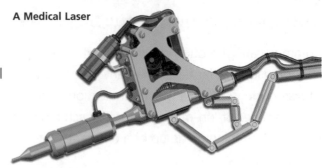

HT Lasers produce an intense beam of light in which all the light waves:

- have the same frequency
- are **in phase** with each other
- do not diverge.

'In phase' means that all the peaks and troughs match up: they go up together and down together. For this to happen the waves must be **monochromatic** and **coherent**. When waves are **in phase** they transmit a lot of energy.

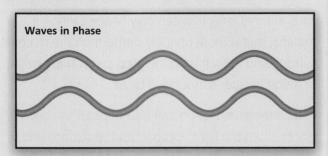

Waves **out of phase** will transmit less overall energy.

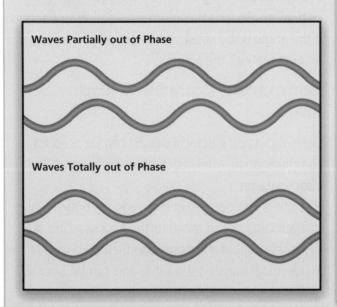

Compact Discs

Digital information can be stored as a sequence of billions of tiny pits (a digital code) in a metal layer on the underside of a compact disc (CD). A CD player spins the disc and laser light is reflected from the pits. The reflected pulses of light (a digital signal of ons and offs) are detected and turned into electrical signals and then transmitted to an amplifier.

Using Signals

Light signals travel very fast and can be sent down optical cables using total internal reflection with only a very small amount of signal loss.

Electrical signals can be sent along wires, but the resistance of the wire causes the signal to deteriorate.

Radio signals can travel through air but are easily lost or weakened in the atmosphere.

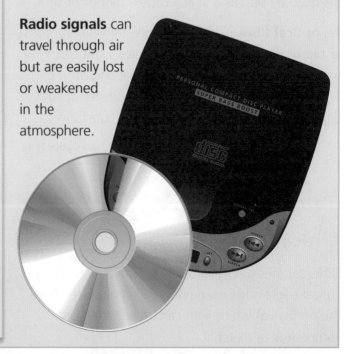

Infrared Cooking

Most cooking still uses **infrared radiation**, such as from a toaster, a hob or an oven. All objects give out infrared radiation, but:

- hotter objects emit more infrared than cooler ones
- black objects emit more infrared than pale ones at the same temperature
- rougher or dull surfaces emit more infrared than shiny ones at the same temperature.

Food in an oven gets hot because it absorbs the infrared that the oven is emitting, but:

- a black object absorbs infrared better than a pale one so gets hotter more easily
- a shiny object reflects infrared so it cannot absorb it and does not get hot so easily.

Wrapping a baked potato in kitchen foil reduces the amount of infrared radiation it emits, so it cools more slowly.

HT When an object absorbs infrared, the energy from the electromagnetic wave is absorbed by the particles in the surface of the object and so their kinetic energy increases (they vibrate more). This means that the temperature of the object will increase. Some surface particles become so hot that they get damaged and become brown (burnt).

The hotter surface particles then transfer energy to particles in the centre by conduction so the whole thing cooks through.

Cooking with Infrared

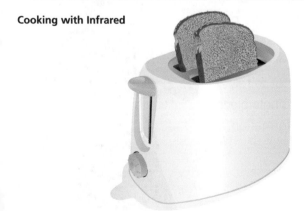

Cooking with Microwaves

Microwaves are electromagnetic waves that can penetrate about 1cm into food and are absorbed by water and fat molecules in the food. Shiny metal surfaces reflect microwaves, which is why you should not put metal objects into a microwave oven. Microwaves can penetrate through glass or plastic so food in containers made from these materials can cook easily.

HT Water and fat molecules in the outer layers of food absorb microwaves very efficiently and the energy increases their kinetic energy, making the material hot. The food should be stirred to enable the heat to be spread through the food.

Because microwaves have longer wavelengths than infrared, they are absorbed by water and fat more easily than infrared. This means they cook food more quickly and are more able to cause burns on body tissue.

Mobile Communicating with Microwaves

Microwaves are used for communication, such as by mobile phones. They can transmit information over large distances that are in **line of sight**, which means that the transmitters and receiver must have no obstacles between them. Some areas are not in line of sight so they have poor signals, which is why your mobile phone may cut out or fail to get a connection.

Microwaves Used for Communication

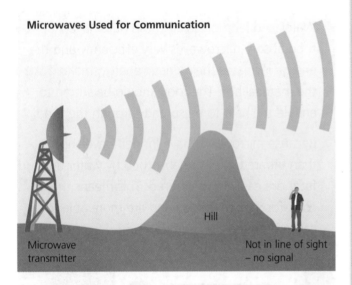

Hill

Microwave transmitter

Not in line of sight – no signal

Sometimes microwave signals are poor. This could be due to:
- a large obstacle such as a building or a mountain
- the signal being affected by the weather or a large area of water
- the curvature of the Earth
- the signal getting weaker as it travels further.

It is possible to try to reduce signal loss by putting transmitters and receivers closer together and by positioning them on high ground so that buildings, hills etc. do not get in the way and so that the curvature of the Earth has less effect.

It is not possible to rely on diffraction of microwaves around buildings, hills etc. because their wavelength is not large enough. It is also impossible to do anything to stop interference between signals.

Microwaves and Health

Mobile phones use microwave signals but they are not the same wavelength as those used in microwave cookers.

There is public concern about children using mobile phones because their skulls are thinner and people think their brains may get damaged by the microwaves. There is also concern about possible dangers to adult users and people who live near transmission masts, even though there is no evidence of any effect on people when thorough tests have been carried out.

There have been many studies into the effect of mobile phones on people. Almost all show that there is no adverse effect on people who use mobile phones or live near phone masts. Some studies show a link between frequent phone use and brain tumours but they do not show that the microwaves from phones or phone masts cause these tumours or any other effect on health.

All the scientific studies into the effects of mobile phones' microwave radiation have been published. This makes it possible to check all the results and compare the conclusions.

There seems to have been conflicting information about the impact of mobile phones or phone masts on people.

It is always important to weigh up the evidence and the potential benefits and risks and make an informed decision, and not to rely on a single piece of information.

Transmitting

Infrared waves can be used for transmitting signals for:

- remote controls for televisions, videos, DVDs etc.
- short distance links between computers and printers, e.g. WiFi.

Infrared sensors, such as those connected to burglar alarms in houses, can detect body heat. When a warm body walks into a room the burglar alarm will go off.

Thermal imaging cameras also detect infrared from bodies and can display an image to show which parts are warm or cold (see page 4).

Signals

There are two types of signal that can be used to transmit data. They are:

- **analogue**
- **digital**.

They each have properties that make them suitable for different uses.

Analogue signals vary continually in amplitude. They can have any value within a fixed range of values and are very similar to the sound waves of speech or music.

Analogue Signal

Digital signals do not vary; they have only two values or states: on (1) or off (0). There are no values in between. The information is a series of pulses.

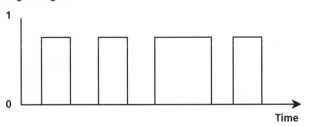
Digital Signal

Remote Controls

When you use a remote control, the device in your hand uses a set of digital signals (or codes) to control each of the different functions.

Advantages of Digital Signals

The big advantage of digital signals is that more information can be transmitted along optical fibres. **Multiplexing** is a technique where two or more digital signals can be carried down the same fibre.

Both digital and analogue signals suffer from interference in the form of noise, but this is easily removable from digital signals leaving them as clear as when they were first sent.

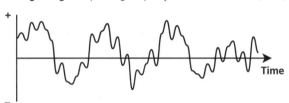
Analogue Signal – poor signal quality due to interference (noise)

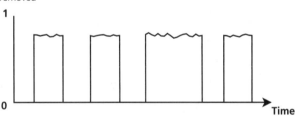
Digital Signal – high signal quality because interference is easily removed

Optical Fibres

Optical fibres have big advantages:

- they allow very rapid transmission of data
- they use light pulses for transmission of data.

The switchover to digital TV from analogue TV means that we will be able to receive more channels because more information can be transmitted by digital signals and images are less likely to be fuzzy or 'noisy' because digital signals do not suffer from interference.

Wireless Signals

Electromagnetic radiation (such as radio waves and microwaves) can be used to send information without optical fibres because it can be reflected and refracted in the same way as visible light. Sometimes this is a disadvantage because it can cause loss of signal.

This **wireless technology** (**WiFi**) is used in **TVs**, **radios**, **mobile phones** and **laptop** computers and has three main advantages:
- No wiring is needed – you do not need to be connected directly to the transmitter.
- It enables items to be portable and convenient.
- It allows access signals on the move.

But you do have to have an aerial to pick up the signals.

Transmitting Signals

Long-distance communication depends on:
- **Reflection** – the **ionosphere** is an electrically charged layer in the Earth's upper atmosphere. **Longer wavelength** radio waves are **reflected** by the ionosphere. This enables radio and television programmes to be transmitted between different places, which may be in different countries or continents around the Earth.
- **Refraction** – at the interfaces of different layers of the Earth's atmosphere, refraction of waves results in the waves changing direction.

Refraction and reflection in the ionosphere act in the same way as total internal reflection for light and keep the signals in the Earth's atmosphere instead of escaping into space.

Negative effects on signal quality include:
- **Diffraction** (changes to the direction and intensity of waves) at the edge of transmission dishes causes the waves to spread out, which results in signal loss. Interference from similar signals limits the distance between transmitters. Positioning transmitters in high places can help to overcome the nuisance of obstacles blocking signals.
- **Refraction** at the interfaces of different layers of the Earth's atmosphere can lead to loss of signal.

If signals are sent to satellites above the atmosphere, the signals can be 'bounced' from satellite to satellite (received and retransmitted) to cover longer distances and travel round the world.

Interference

Some signals have a poorer quality than others so sometimes the information is 'noisy' (see page 15) and you get hissing, called **interference**. Another form of interference can happen if there are two radio stations using similar frequencies. The two stations can cause mutual interference so that you hear parts of one programme on top of the other.

Interference cannot happen with digital signals because each station has a transmission frequency that is well separated from all others (each station requires less bandwidth so there is more space) and the processing enables random signals to be filtered out before they are turned into sound or light.

DAB

Some radio stations provide better signals than others. Analogue signals often suffer from interference. **DAB (Digital Audio Broadcasting)** uses digital signals. The advantages are:
- more stations can be transmitted
- there is less interference between stations.

But there are some disadvantages to DAB:
- The audio quality is poorer than with **FM** (frequency modulated signals – analogue).
- Not all areas of the country are covered so you may be driving along and pass into an area where there is no signal.

Earthquakes

Earthquakes produce shock waves that can travel inside the Earth and across the surface and cause damage to buildings and the Earth's surface. These waves are called **seismic waves** and can be detected by **seismometers** and recorded on **seismographs**. There are two types of seismic wave:

- **P-waves** (primary waves) are longitudinal and travel through both solids and liquids.
- **S-waves** (secondary waves) are transverse waves and travel through solids but not through liquids. They travel more slowly than P-waves.

Earthquakes can also cause tsunamis.

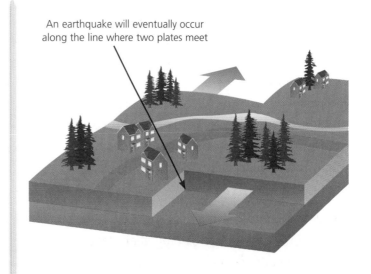

An earthquake will eventually occur along the line where two plates meet

The properties of seismic waves provide evidence for the structure of the Earth. After an earthquake occurs, the waves are detected all over the world as shown in the diagram. P-waves can travel through the liquid outer core so they are detected in most places. S-waves will not pass through liquids so they are only detected closer to the **epicentre** (the centre of the earthquake).

Primary Waves (P-waves)

Primary waves are longitudinal waves: the vibrations are in the same direction as the wave is travelling. They can travel through solids and liquids and through all the layers of the Earth.

Secondary Waves (S-waves)

Secondary waves are transverse waves: the vibrations are at right angles to the direction the wave is travelling. They can travel through solids but not liquids. They cannot travel through the Earth's outer (liquid) core and are slower than primary waves.

A study of seismic waves indicates that the Earth is made up of:

- a thin crust
- a mantle which is semi-fluid and extends almost halfway to the centre
- a core which is over half of the Earth's diameter with a liquid outer part and a solid inner part.

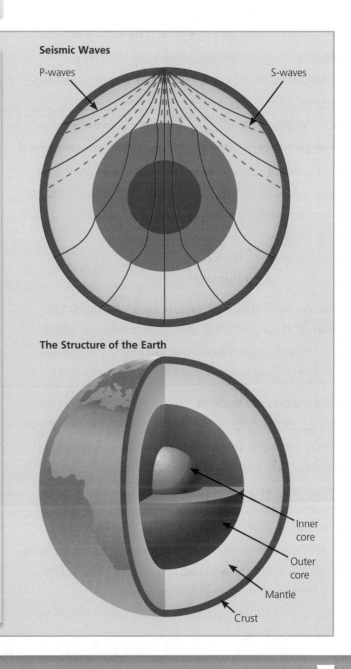

Seismic Waves

P-waves   S-waves

The Structure of the Earth

Inner core

Outer core

Mantle

Crust

Dangerous Sun

The Sun is responsible for life on Earth but it can also be very damaging. One kind of electromagnetic wave produced by the Sun is called **ultraviolet radiation** which can give a sun tan. However, prolonged exposure can cause **premature skin ageing**, **sunburn** or **skin cancer**, and **cataracts** in the eyes of older people. Some people are suffering from skin cancer as a result of using sunbeds.

People with darker skin are less at risk because their skin absorbs more ultraviolet radiation, meaning less reaches the underlying body tissue.

Sunscreen is also effective at reducing the damage caused by ultraviolet radiation. The higher the **factor**, the lower the risk because high factor sunscreens allow longer exposure without burning:

> Safe time = Recommended exposure time × Sunblock factor

On a bright sunny day in England it is advised that you spend no more than 20 minutes in the midday Sun. By wearing a factor 2 sunblock you can double this time:
Safe time = 20 minutes × 2
= **40 minutes**

Factor 3 will triple the time you can spend in the Sun, and so on. Factor 30 should keep you safe for 10 hours, which should see you safely through a whole day, as long as you keep reapplying it.

The media and doctors have put a lot of effort into informing people of the dangers, with campaigns to persuade us to use sunscreens, not to stay out in the midday Sun and not to use sunbeds.

Ozone Depletion

Ozone is a gas found naturally high up in the Earth's atmosphere – it prevents too many harmful ultraviolet (UV) rays reaching the Earth. Recently, scientists noticed that the **ozone layer** is becoming thinner and that there was a 'hole' near the South Pole.

To be certain that this was a real effect and not simply an error, they have repeated the readings with new equipment and other scientists have also taken the same measurements. Scientists have also made predictions, based on their explanation of how the ozone hole was formed, and then tested their predictions to show that their explanations are reliable.

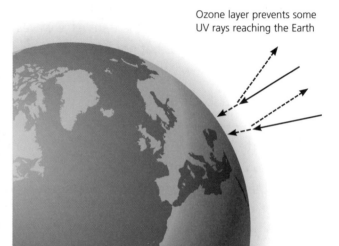

Ozone layer prevents some UV rays reaching the Earth

Scientists think that **CFCs** (chlorofluorocarbons) in factories, fridges and aerosol cans have caused this change in the ozone layer. They have tested this idea by looking at how ozone is affected by different chemicals and also to see for how long CFCs remain in the upper atmosphere. As a result of their work CFCs have been banned in most countries. Scientists are continuing to measure the ozone levels, which do vary every year. The prediction is that the ozone layer will eventually repair itself.

Scientists are also noting that more people are suffering from skin cancer in the Southern Hemisphere. This fits with the observation that the ozone layer is important in protecting people from ultraviolet radiation. There have been many campaigns to educate people to use sunscreens. People are now more likely to use sunscreen and less likely to get sunburnt.

1 Sarah is eating an ice lolly in the Sun and the ice lolly starts to melt. The graph shows the change in temperature of the ice lolly over time.

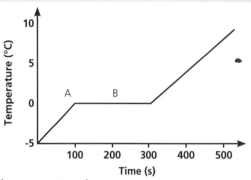

a) What is happening at point B? Put a tick (✓) next to the correct option. [1]

Sarah has finished the ice lolly ☐	Sarah has gone inside, out of the sun ☐
The ice lolly is melting ☐	The ice lolly is freezing ☐

b) Specific heat capacity is the energy needed to raise the temperature of 1kg of a material by 1°C. The mass of the ice lolly is 57g and the specific heat capacity is 1.34 kJ/kg/°C. Use this information, and the graph above to calculate the energy transferred to the ice lolly before point A. [1]

2 Helen wants to insulate her house. She has collected some information about different types of house insulation, as shown in the table.

Method of Insulation	Cost	Annual Saving	Payback Time
Double glazing	£2100	£70	
Draught excluders	£30	£20	
Fibreglass loft insulation	£500	£25	

a) Fill in the table by calculating the payback time for each method of insulation. [3]

b) Use the information in the table to suggest which type of insulation Helen should choose. Explain your answer. [1]

HT c) Because her house has been so cold recently, Helen has been putting silver foil on the walls behind the radiators. How might this have helped to keep the house warm? [3]

3 Mobile phones are an example of the use of wireless technology.

a) What type of electromagnetic wave do mobile phones use? [1]

b) A mobile phone signal has a wavelength of 2cm. What is the frequency of the wave? [2]

c) There are plans for the construction of a new mobile phone mast in a town due to poor mobile phone signals in the area. The picture shows the location of the town. Identify the likely reason why there is bad signal and explain why this would cause the problem. [2]

d) There have been a number of complaints from local residents about the mobile phone mast. State one advantage and one disadvantage of this new construction. [2]

P2: Living for the Future (Energy Resources)

This module looks at:
- The Sun and solar energy.
- How electricity is generated in power stations and transported.
- Global warming and the greenhouse effect.
- Sources of heat energy for power stations and their economic and environmental factors.
- Radioactivity, ionising radiation and safety factors related to radioactivity.
- The objects that make up our Solar System and the Universe, and problems with space exploration.
- The threat of an asteroid collision with Earth.
- Theories about how the Universe was formed and its future.

The Sun

The Sun is a stable source of energy that transfers energy to the Earth in the form of light and heat.

Photocells

A **photocell** (sometimes called a solar cell) has a flat surface that captures as much of the light energy from the Sun as possible.

It transfers this light energy into an electric current that travels in the same direction all the time (**direct current, DC**).

The power output of the photocells depends on the surface area exposed to the sunlight, so lots of photocells can be joined together to create a larger surface and therefore increase the amount of light captured from the Sun.

The advantages and disadvantages of photocells are listed in the table.

Advantages
- Require little maintenance once installed.
- Can operate in remote locations to give access to electricity without installing power cables.
- No need for fuel because the Sun is the source of energy.
- Have a long life.
- Use energy from the Sun, which is a renewable energy source.
- No pollution or waste produced.

Disadvantages
- Expensive to buy.
- No power at night or during bad weather.

How Photocells Work

The Sun's energy is absorbed by the photocell, causing **electrons** to be knocked loose from the silicon crystals. These electrons flow freely as an electric current. This flow of charge is called an **electric current**.

The power of a photocell depends on the surface area exposed to the light, the distance from the light source and the **intensity** of that source. (Intensity means how concentrated the light energy is.)

To maximise power output, an efficient solar collector must track (follow) the Sun in the sky. This requires additional technology, which increases the initial set-up cost.

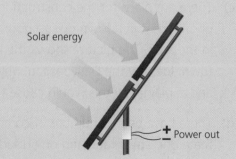

Solar energy

Power out

Harnessing the Sun's Energy

Light from the Sun (radiation) can be captured and used in other ways too.

Sunlight can be absorbed by the surface of a solar panel and transferred into heat energy. Water passed over this surface will be heated to a reasonable temperature and can be used for washing and for heating buildings.

Flat plate collector – solar panel filled with water

Hot water to house

Cold water supply

Heat exchanger

Water tank

Pump

A **curved mirror** can be used to focus the Sun's light, rather like a magnifying glass, to heat up a solar panel.

Glass can be used to provide **passive solar heating** for buildings. 'Passive solar heating' simply means a device that traps energy from the Sun (e.g. a greenhouse) but that does not distribute the energy or change it into another form of energy. This is what causes conservatories to get so hot in the summer.

> **HT** Glass is transparent to some wavelengths of the Sun's radiation, including visible light – so light passes straight through glass windows and is absorbed by objects in the room. The heated surfaces then emit infrared radiation (longer wavelength than visible light), which is reflected back into the room by the glass so cannot escape. This warms up the room.

Wind Turbines

The Sun heats up the air and causes convection currents – the wind. **Wind turbines** depend on the wind produced by the Sun's energy. Wind turbines transfer the **kinetic energy** (**KE**) of the air into **electrical energy**.

The advantages and disadvantages of wind turbines are listed below.

Advantages
• Wind is a **renewable** energy source so it will not run out.
• There is no chemical **pollution** or **waste**.

Disadvantages
• Wind turbines require a large amount of **space** in a windy region to deliver a reasonable amount of electricity.
• They are **dependent** on the wind – no wind means no electricity.
• They cause **visual pollution** because they are very big.

The Dynamo Effect

Electricity can be generated by moving a wire, or a coil of wire, near a magnet (or by moving the magnet near to the wire). When this happens the wire cuts through the lines of force of the magnetic field and a current is produced in the wire, providing it is part of a **complete circuit**.

Electricity can be generated by moving a magnet towards a coil of wire.

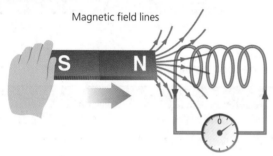

Magnetic field lines

Electricity can also be generated by moving the coil of wire towards the magnet.

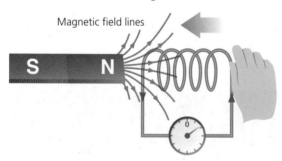

Magnetic field lines

The current generated can be increased by:
• using a stronger magnet
• using more turns of wire in the coil
• moving the coil (or magnet) faster.

Generators use the dynamo effect to produce electricity. **Batteries** produce a **direct current** (DC) but generators produce an **alternating current** (AC). This means that the direction of the current is continually alternating (changing direction) as time passes, every time the magnet (or coil) changes direction.

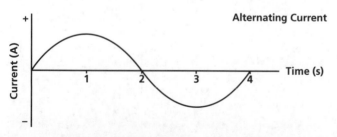

Alternating Current

The graph shows that as time passes, the line curves up and down again. This means that the current alternates from a positive direction (forward) to a negative one (backward) and back again.

The **voltage** generated changes direction and this causes the current to change direction giving alternating current (AC).

N.B. It is also possible to plot the voltage of AC against time.

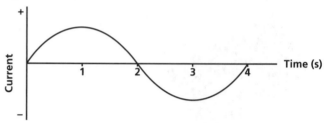

How an AC Generator Works

In an AC generator, a coil of wire is rotated in a magnetic field. In practice, the coil and magnetic field should be close together. As the coil cuts through the magnetic field a current is generated in the coil. The current alternates, i.e. it reverses direction of flow every half turn of the coil, as can be seen below.

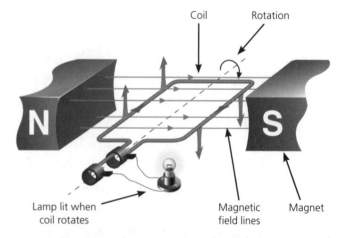

Lamp lit when coil rotates / Magnetic field lines / Magnet / Coil / Rotation

Position of Coil to Generate Current in the AC Cycle

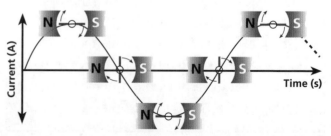

Producing Electricity

The heat energy for our power stations comes from a variety of energy sources. Electricity is transmitted to consumers (homes, factories, offices, farms, etc.) through the network of cables called the **National Grid**, which connects the power stations to consumers.

Fossil fuels such as crude oil, coal and natural gas can be burned to release heat energy, which boils water to produce steam. The steam rotates the turbines, which turn the generators, which produce electricity.

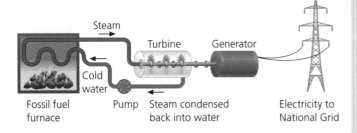

Fossil fuel furnace | Pump | Steam condensed back into water | Electricity to National Grid

In a **nuclear power station** there are fuel rods of uranium (or sometimes plutonium). They release energy (fission) as heat to make steam in the power station.

Biomass such as wood, straw and manure, can be burned or else fermented to generate methane (a gas) that can be burned in a power station.

Biomass such as wood absorbs carbon dioxide as it grows and then releases it when burned so the amount of CO_2 in the atmosphere remains constant. However, biomass requires very large areas of land to produce enough material to generate significant amounts of energy. This land could be used to grow food instead.

Fossil fuels are readily available now but supplies are running out. They also produce **pollution** including carbon dioxide (CO_2) which is a **greenhouse gas** and contributes to climate change.

Efficiency of a Power Station

A significant amount of energy produced by conventional power stations is wasted. At each stage in the electricity generation process, energy is transferred to the surroundings in a 'non-useful' form, usually as heat.

Below is a typical energy transfer diagram for the process that shows how much energy is wasted at each stage. Only 30J is used usefully; 70J is wasted (also see page 7).

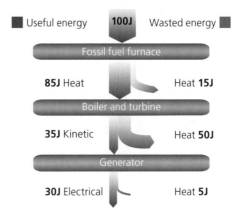

The efficiency of a power station can be worked out as:

$$\text{Efficiency} = \frac{\text{Useful energy output}}{\text{Total energy input}} \times 100\%$$

HT The following equations are also used when calculating the efficiency of a power station:

$$\text{Fuel energy input (J)} = \text{Waste energy output (J)} + \text{Electrical energy output (J)}$$

$$\text{Efficiency} = \frac{\text{Electrical energy output (J)}}{\text{Fuel energy input (J)}} \times 100\%$$

Example

A power station uses 200 000J of fuel energy to produce 80 000J of electrical energy.

a) What is the waste energy output?

Rearrange the first formula:

$$\text{Waste energy output} = \text{Fuel energy input} - \text{Electrical energy output}$$

$$= 200\,000J - 80\,000J$$

$$= \textbf{120\,000J}$$

b) What is the efficiency of this power station?

$$\text{Efficiency} = \frac{\text{Electrical energy output}}{\text{Fuel energy input}} \times 100\%$$

$$= \frac{80\,000J}{200\,000J} \times 100\%$$

$$= 0.4 \times 100\% = \textbf{40\%}$$

The Greenhouse Effect

There are some gases in the Earth's atmosphere that do not allow heat to escape (radiate) into space. This causes the Earth to warm up in the same way that the glass in a greenhouse makes the greenhouse warm up on a sunny day. This warming up is called the **greenhouse effect**.

The greenhouse effect happens because some wavelengths of the electromagnetic spectrum cannot pass through the atmosphere – in particular, longer wavelength infrared rays are absorbed by some gases in the atmosphere – while all the rest can.

Greenhouse Gases

Some examples of greenhouse gases are:
- carbon dioxide
- water vapour
- methane.

All of these gases occur naturally in the atmosphere but are also man-made (i.e. produced through the activities of humans).

Water vapour

Carbon dioxide

How Does the Atmosphere Heat Up?

Short wavelength radiation from the Sun, such as visible light, infrared and ultraviolet, can pass through the atmosphere. This radiation is then absorbed by Earth and heats it.

The Earth is cooler than the Sun so it emits longer wavelength infrared rays that cannot pass through the atmosphere. Instead they are absorbed by the greenhouse gases in the atmosphere, which then heats up.

Methane (produced by cows and by growing rice) is a very powerful greenhouse gas – it absorbs four times as much heat as carbon dioxide. However, carbon dioxide levels are rising much faster than water vapour or methane levels because carbon dioxide is produced by the burning of fossil fuels for heat or to generate electricity, so carbon dioxide is considered to be the biggest cause of global warming.

In examinations you may be expected to interpret data about the abundance and impact of greenhouse gases.

Climate Change

The world is using much more energy than ever before. To generate this energy we need to burn more fossil fuels, and this produces more greenhouse gases such as carbon dioxide. This may be why the Earth is warming up.

Trees can absorb carbon dioxide but humans are cutting down trees (**deforestation**) so the carbon dioxide levels just keep rising and the Earth continues to warm up.

As the Earth warms up, the wind and weather patterns across the globe change – climate change.

Changing weather patterns mean there is more **rainfall** and **flooding** in some countries, more **hurricanes** in other countries and less rainfall and more **droughts** in others (it is not just about everywhere getting warmer!). This is called **climate change**.

Reasons for Climate Change

Human activity and natural phenomena seem to affect the climate:

- Humans burning fossil fuels causes an increase in the greenhouse gases in the atmosphere.
- Dust from factories can reflect heat from cities back to the Earth.
- Dust from volcanic ash clouds can reflect radiation from the Sun back into space and cause the Earth's temperature to fall.

Evidence for Climate Change

Scientists have been measuring the Earth's temperature over many centuries, but it is not easy. Although we can use thermometers today, no one used thermometers to measure the Earth's temperature hundreds of years ago. So scientists have to look at other evidence for the Earth's temperature many years ago, such as the thickness of tree rings in old timbers – if the Earth was warm in a particular year the trees grew more and so the tree ring is thicker.

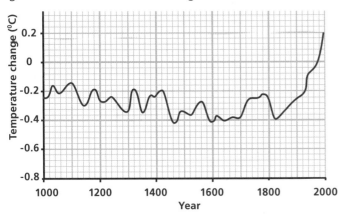

Scientists all over the world are measuring the temperature in thousands of different locations to try to decide if the average temperature is still changing. Of course each different location gives a different answer so it's important that scientists share their data with each other.

The evidence so far seems to show that the Earth has warmed up significantly over the past 200 years. Scientists consider that this trend will continue and predict that the Earth's temperature will continue to increase.

Some people do not believe the evidence because they notice that the local weather is not improving. They mix up the evidence with their own opinion. They forget that scientists use thousands of thermometers and take averages across the world, whereas these people just see the effect on one tiny part of the world.

Scientists in Disagreement

The aim of every scientist is to look critically at other scientists' work to see if it is correct and to point out when it is not. This is how errors in science are found and removed and how science moves forward. If scientists did not do this then science would be far less reliable.

Scientists always take data seriously and will look at every possible way that the data can be interpreted to be sure that they all agree on the correct interpretation. Scientists certainly do not 'take another person's word for it'. Climate change has made scientists work harder than ever to be sure that the data are correct and that the interpretation is agreed.

So far it seems that the data do show that the Earth is warming up and experiments show clearly that greenhouse gases contribute to this. This is where scientists agree.

Some scientists have pointed out that there may be other interpretations of the data on what causes the temperature to rise – could it be Sun spots? Or something that happens on a thousand-year cycle? There is still work to be done to find out if human activity is the main cause of the temperature rising.

In the exam you may be expected to interpret data about increased global warming and climate change as a result of human activity.

Power and Energy Transfer in Circuits

An **electric current** involves a flow of electric charge which transfers energy from the battery or power supply to the components in the circuit. If the component is a light bulb then some of the electrical energy is transformed into light.

The rate of this energy transfer determines the power of the component or device and is measured in joules per second or **watts** (W), where 1 watt is the transfer of 1 joule of energy in 1 second.

Electrical power is calculated using the relationship:

| Power (W) | = | Current (A) | × | Voltage (V) | $\dfrac{P}{I \times V}$ |

where *I* is current

Example

Calculate the power of a lamp when the current flowing through it is 0.3A and the voltage across it is 3V. Using the formula:

Power = Current × Voltage

$\qquad$ = 0.3A × 3V

$\qquad$ **= 0.9W**

This means that the lamp transfers 0.9 joules of electrical energy in every second that it is switched on. The power rating of a device is usually written on it in watts (W) or in kilowatts (kW). One kW is 1000W.

HT Example

Calculate the current flowing through a 900W iron when it is being used at its maximum power and working voltage (230V). Rearrange the formula:

$$\text{Current} = \frac{\text{Power}}{\text{Voltage}}$$

$$= \frac{900W}{230V}$$

$$= 3.9A$$

HT Off-Peak Electricity

Electricity is supplied to our homes 24 hours a day. It is often our preferred source of energy because no smoke or gases are produced in the home. However, the electricity is generated using fossil fuels that do produce pollution so the consumer is still, indirectly, adding to the damage being caused to the environment.

Most electricity is used when people are awake and active. There is obviously less demand during the night. However, it is not easy to switch a power station off so power stations generate electricity all the time. (Electricity is produced as you use it – it cannot be stored). In order to encourage people to use the electricity generated during this quiet period, some electricity-generating companies offer cheaper electricity at night called **off-peak electricity**. This can be used for:

* heating up water and storage heaters
* powering washing machines and dishwashers running at night.

The advantage for electricity-generating companies is that they can sell the electricity they generate and do not have to switch off the power stations. The advantage for the consumer is that the cost is lower. The disadvantage to the consumer is that it is inconvenient to run appliances at night because of the noise. The disadvantage to the producer is that they make less profit.

Electricity Meters

Your electricity meter at home will look similar to the one shown. It will show a count of **Units**. These Units represent **kilowatt hours** (kWh), which are a measure of how much electrical energy has been used.

Kilowatt Hours

The number of Units of electricity used by an appliance depends on:
- the power rating in kilowatts of the appliance
- the time in hours that the appliance is switched on for.

To calculate the **cost** of using a device, use the formulae:

(Energy supplied) Number of kilowatt-hours (kWh)	=	Power rating (kW)	×	Time (h)

Total cost	=	Number of kilowatt-hours (kWh)	×	Cost of one kWh

Example

A 1.5kW electric hot plate was switched on for 2 hours. How much does the electricity used cost if electricity is 8p per kWh?

First, calculate the number of kilowatt hours used, using the formula:

Number of kWh = Power × Time
= 1.5kW × 2h = **3kWh**

Then, calculate the cost:

Total cost = Number of kWh used × Cost per Unit
= 3 × 8p = **24p**

 Measuring Energy Supplied

The kilowatt hour is a measure of how much electricity has been used. It is also a measure of how much electrical energy has been supplied.

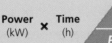 Energy supplied (kWh) = Power (kW) × Time (h)

Example 1
A 200W CD player is used for 90 minutes. Calculate the energy supplied.

 Using the formula:

Energy supplied = Power × Time
= 0.2kW × 1.5h
= **0.3kWh**

> Power must be in kW and time must be in h.

Example 2
On a building site, 2.25kWh of electrical energy is supplied to an electric drill in 3 hours. What is the power rating of the electric drill?

Rearrange the formula:

$$Power = \frac{Energy\ supplied}{Time}$$

$$= \frac{2.25kWh}{3h}$$

= **0.75kW or 750W**

N.B. To do these calculations, you must always remember to make sure the power is in kilowatts and the time is in hours.

Transformers

To supply electricity to our homes efficiently across the **National Grid** the current is fed through **transformers**.

A transformer can increase the voltage of the supply (and at the same time reduce the current). A transformer can also reduce the voltage of a supply.

Increasing the voltage has the effect of reducing the energy lost as heat as the electricity is transmitted and so reduces the costs.

Using a transformer to increase the voltage of the supply will result in the current decreasing. If the current through the cables is lower then there is less heating ($P = I^2R$). This means that there is less energy wasted as heat in the cable and so the process of transmission is more efficient and less costly.

Comparing Fuel and Energy Sources

The table below lists the advantages and disadvantages of different types of fuel and renewable energy sources. Fossil fuels, biomass and nuclear fuels are commonly used in power stations.

Source	Advantages	Disadvantages
Fossil fuel, e.g. coal, oil, gas	• Enough reserves for short to medium term. • Relatively cheap and easy to obtain. • Coal-, oil- and gas-fired power stations are flexible in meeting demand and have a relatively short start-up time. • Burning gas produces very little SO_2 (sulfur dioxide).	• Produces CO_2 that causes global warming and SO_2 (except burning gas) that causes acid rain. • Removing SO_2 from waste gases to reduce acid rain, and removing CO_2 to reduce global warming, adds to the cost. • Oil is often carried between continents in tankers, leading to risk of spillage and pollution. • Expensive pipelines and networks are often required to transport oil and gas to the point of use.
Biomass, e.g. wood, straw, manure	• It is renewable. • Can be burned to produce heat. • Fermenting biomass produces methane, which can be burned.	• Produces CO_2 which damages the environment. • Large area needed to grow trees which could be used for other purposes, e.g. growing food.
Nuclear fuel, e.g. uranium	• Cost and rate of fuel use is relatively low. • Can be situated in sparsely populated areas. • Nuclear power stations are flexible in meeting demand. • Does not produce CO_2 or SO_2. • High stocks of nuclear fuel. • Can reduce the use of fossil fuels.	• Radioactive material can stay dangerously radioactive for thousands of years and can be harmful. • Storing radioactive waste is very expensive. • Building and decommissioning nuclear power stations are costly. • Comparatively long start-up time. • Radioactive material could be emitted. • Pollution from fuel processing. • High maintenance costs.
Renewable sources, e.g. wind, tidal, hydroelectric, solar	• No fuel costs during operation. • No chemical pollution. • Often low labour costs. • Do not contribute to global warming or produce acid rain. • Produce clean electricity. • Can be constructed in remote areas.	• With the exception of hydroelectric, they produce small amounts of electricity. • Take up lots of space and are unsightly. • Unreliable (apart from hydroelectric), depend on the weather and cannot guarantee supply on demand. • High initial costs to build and install. • High maintenance costs.

Types of Radiation

Radioactive materials are substances that give out nuclear radiation all the time, regardless of what is done to them.

Nuclear radiation is often used in medical treatments such as **radiotherapy** to cure cancer. This works because the nuclear radiation can kill the cancer cells. However, the radiotherapists have to be careful as the nuclear radiation can also kill healthy cells.

Radioactivity involves a change in the structure of the radioactive atom and the release of one of the three types of nuclear radiation:

- **alpha** (α)
- **beta** (β)
- **gamma** (γ).

Nuclear radiation can cause **ionisation**, producing positively and negatively charged ions when atoms lose or gain electrons. Ionisation can be harmful inside the body – it damages cells and can initiate chemical reactions by breaking molecular bonds.

Use of Alpha Radiation

Most **smoke detectors** contain americium-241, which emits alpha radiation. The emitted alpha particles cause the **ionisation** of air particles. The positive and negative ions formed are attracted to oppositely charged electrodes in the detector. This results in a current flowing in the circuit.

When smoke enters the space between the two electrodes, less ionisation takes place because the alpha particles are absorbed by the smoke particles. A smaller current then flows, and the alarm sounds.

Uses of Beta Radiation

A **tracer** is a small amount of a radioactive substance that is put into a system so that its progress through the system can be followed using a radiation detector. A beta-emitter tracer can be used for the following:

- To detect tumours in certain parts of a patient's body, e.g. brain, lungs.

- To identify plants that have been fed with a fertiliser containing a beta particle emitter. (This method can be used to develop better fertilisers.)
- In a **paper thickness gauge**. When beta radiation passes through paper, some of it is absorbed. The greater the thickness of the paper, the greater the absorption. If the paper thickness is too great, then more beta radiation is absorbed, and less passes through to the detector. A signal is then sent to the rollers to move closer together, which reduces the thickness of the paper.

Uses of Gamma Radiation

Gamma radiation can be used to **treat cancer** because it destroys cancerous cells. A high, calculated dose is aimed at the tumour (cancer) from many different angles so that only cancerous cells are destroyed, and not healthy cells.

Gamma radiation can also be used to **sterilise medical equipment** because it can destroy microorganisms – for example, bacteria. An advantage of this method is that no heat is required, which minimises the damage to equipment that heat might cause.

Non-destructive tests can be carried out on welds using gamma radiation. A gamma source is placed on one side, and any cracks or defects can be identified using a detector (e.g. photographic film) on the other side as the gamma rays get through.

Radiation and Cancer

Radiation, including radiation from radioactive waste from **hospitals** and **power stations**, can affect living cells and can cause cancer. It is not a pollutant and does not contribute to global warming.

Dealing with Radioactive Waste Materials

Some radioactive waste can be reprocessed, but often it has to be disposed of. Low-level waste is sealed and buried in landfill sites. High-level waste is mixed with sugar, bonded with glass, poured into a steel cylinder and kept underground.

How to Test Penetrating Power

To test the **penetrating power** of alpha, beta and gamma radiation, a **Geiger counter** can be set up to detect the radiation. Each radioactive source is placed so that its radioactive decay particles can be detected by the Geiger counter. Different materials are then inserted, as in the diagram below.

The diagram below shows each type of radiation's penetrative power, i.e. what materials the radiation can pass through.

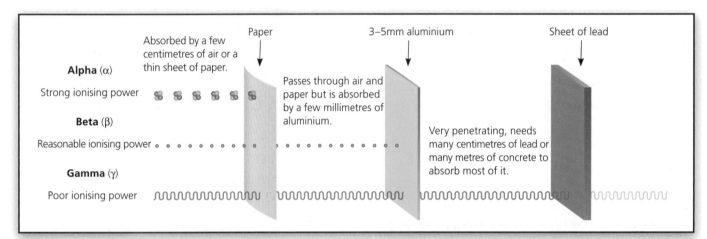

Handling Radioactive Materials Safely

There are four main **safety measures** that need to be taken by people who handle radioactive materials:

- Protective clothing must be worn.
- Tongs should be used to hold the material whenever possible.
- Exposure time should be minimised.
- Radioactive materials must be stored in clearly labelled, shielded containers so that others are aware of what they are handling.

Nuclear Power and Radiation

Nuclear power stations use **uranium** fuel rods to release energy as heat. Uranium, like coal, is a non-renewable resource so it will run out one day, but it does not cause global warming because it does not release carbon dioxide.

One of the waste products from nuclear reactors is **plutonium**, which can be used to make **nuclear bombs.**

HT Advantages and Disadvantages of Nuclear Power

Advantage
Does not emit polluting gases such as carbon dioxide so does not contribute to the greenhouse effect.

Disadvantage
Waste is radioactive so has to be treated and stored for many years.

Problems of Dealing with Radioactive Waste

Some of the problems of dealing with radioactive waste include:

- The waste can remain radioactive for many years.
- Terrorists may try to use it to build dirty bombs.
- It has to be stored carefully to ensure that it does not enter the water supply.
- Acceptable radioactivity levels may change over time so measures may need modifying.

The Universe

The Universe consists of:

- **planets, comets** and **meteors**
- **stars** – our Sun is a star. Stars can be clearly seen, even though they are far away, because they are very hot and give out light
- **galaxies**, which are large groups of stars
- **black holes**, which are dense, dead stars with a very strong gravitational field.

The Solar System

The **Solar System** is made up of the Sun (which is in the centre) surrounded by planets, comets and satellites. The Moon is a natural satellite that orbits the Earth.

Relative Sizes

Planets vary in size but they are all bigger than **meteors** (shooting stars).

Comets are bigger than meteors and have a core of frozen gas and dust. They are up to 20km in diameter. A comet's tail is formed by the core evaporating in the sunlight and always points away from the Sun.

HT The eight planets move around the Sun in paths called **orbits**, which are slightly squashed circles (**ellipses**).

The planets, comets and satellites are kept in their orbits by the **gravitational force** of the larger body they are orbiting. Gravity provides the centripetal force needed to prevent the planets from flying off.

Elliptical Orbits

The planets and satellites travel in circular (or near circular) paths around a larger object. Comets travel in elliptical orbits.

They stay in their orbits because the larger object exerts an **inward pull force** on them. This inward pull force is due to **gravity** and is called the **centripetal force**, e.g. the Earth orbits the Sun because of the Sun's gravitational force.

The Sun and the Planets in the Solar System

Sun

Mercury

Venus

Earth

Mars

Jupiter

Saturn

Uranus

Neptune

Pluto

Not to scale

Pluto has been known as a dwarf planet since September 2006.

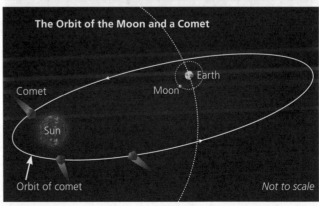

The Orbit of the Moon and a Comet

Comet

Earth

Moon

Sun

Orbit of comet

Not to scale

Relative Sizes (cont)

Stars are much bigger and (except the Sun) are outside of our Solar System. The nearest is *Proxima centauri* which is approximately 4.2 light years away from us.

A **light year** is the distance that light travels in a year. The light year is a useful unit for measuring astronomical distances.

Manned Space Travel

Space is a very dangerous place. There are many difficulties facing a **manned space mission** to the planets:

- The planets are very, very far away so it takes months or even years to reach them.
- The fuel required takes up most of the spacecraft.
- Room must be found to store enough food, water and oxygen for the whole journey.
- A stable artificial atmosphere must be maintained in the spacecraft.
- The temperature in space is about –270°C, so keeping warm is vitally important.
- Outside of the Earth's magnetic field, humans need shielding from cosmic rays.
- The low gravity affects people's health, making muscles weak.
- Radio signals carrying messages take a very long time to reach home.

Unmanned Space Travel

A far more realistic option is to explore our Solar System using **unmanned spaceships**. As well as being able to withstand conditions that are lethal to humans, unmanned probes would not require food, water or oxygen. Once they arrive, probes could be used to send back information about the planet's:

- temperature
- magnetic field
- radiation levels
- gravity
- atmosphere
- surrounding landscape.

However, they cannot bring back samples for analysis.

HT Once the probe arrives on a planet, it can send information to Earth using radio waves which travel at the **speed of light**.

There are many advantages and disadvantages of using **unmanned** spacecraft to explore the Solar System. For example, lower costs – no need to provide food and other things for passengers, and there is also no problem with safety.

However, **reliability** has to be high because there will be no-one to fix any breakdowns, and instruments must require **zero maintenance**.

The Earth and Moon

The Moon may be formed from the remains of a planet that collided with the Earth billions of years ago. If this happened then:

- the planets collided
- the iron cores merged to form the core of the Earth
- the less dense material flew off and now orbits the Earth – it is our Moon.

> **HT** Evidence exists that the Moon may be formed from the remains of a planet that collided with Earth. The Moon is made mainly of rock with no iron core, and this rock appears to have been baked, which would indicate heat generated in a collision.

Asteroids

Asteroids are rocks left over from the formation of the Solar System. They normally orbit the Sun in a belt between Mars and Jupiter, but occasionally they get knocked off course and head towards Earth.

When an asteroid collides with the Earth there can be several devastating consequences:

- The impact forms a crater, which could trigger the ejection of **hot rocks**.
- The heat may cause widespread **fires**.
- Sunlight could be blocked out by the **dust** from the explosion.
- **Climate** change.
- Whole species could become **extinct**, which could, in turn, affect other species.

There is good evidence to suggest that asteroids have collided with the Earth many times in the past:

- **Craters** can be found all over the planet.
- There are layers of unusual **elements** found in rocks.
- There are sudden changes in the number of **fossils** found in adjacent rock layers, which could be due to the sudden death of many animals.

> **HT** There is an asteroid belt between Jupiter and Mars. The asteroids (small lumps of rock) could combine to form a planet but Jupiter's strong gravitational pull prevents them from doing this.

Comets

A **comet** is a small body with a core of frozen gas and dust – like a dirty snowball – which comes from the objects orbiting the Sun far beyond the planets. Their characteristic tails are a trail of debris.

Comets have highly elliptical orbits around the Sun. The speed of the comet increases as it approaches the Sun due to the pull of the Sun's gravity.

> **HT** The comet's speed increases as a result of the increase in the strength of gravity as it approaches the star that it is orbiting. It can also be affected by the gravity of planets.

Near Earth Objects (NEOs)

A **Near Earth Object** (NEO) is an asteroid or comet on a possible **collision course** with Earth. **Telescopes** are used to observe these objects in an attempt to determine their **trajectories** (probable paths). It is difficult to observe NEOs because they move very quickly and there are so many of them (and many artificial satellites in orbit around the Earth).

> **HT** NEOs may pose a threat to the human race but there are actions we can take to reduce that threat. We can:
> - **survey** the skies with telescopes to identify likely NEOs as early as possible
> - **monitor** their progress with satellites
> - **deflect** the object with an explosion if a collision does seem likely.

The Big Bang Theory

One theory that has been used to explain the evolution of the Universe to its present state is the **Big Bang** theory, which states that the whole Universe started billions of years ago in one place with a huge explosion, i.e. a big bang.

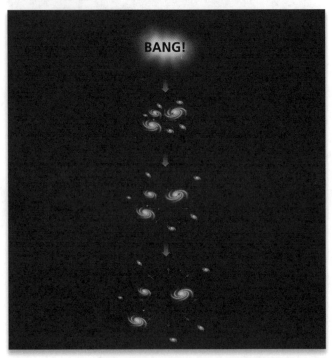

BANG!

The Universe is still expanding after this big explosion. This means that all the galaxies (clusters of stars) are still moving away from us. Scientists have worked out that the furthest galaxies are moving away from us fastest.

We also observe that **microwave radiation** is received from all parts of the Universe.

> **HT** By tracking the movement of the galaxies, we can estimate the **age** and **starting point** of the Universe.
>
> Evidence for the expansion has also been obtained by the measurement of **red-shift**. If a source of light moves away from us, the wavelengths of the light in its spectrum are longer than if the source were not moving. This effect is known as red-shift because the wavelengths are shifted towards the red end of the spectrum.

HT Scientists have noted that the light from more distant galaxies is more red-shifted than light from nearer galaxies. This is evidence for the Universe continuing to expand and for galaxies further away moving faster than those closer to us.

By working out how far the light is red-shifted we can work out the different speeds of the galaxies. We can then work backwards to see when the Big Bang happened to give us an estimate of the age of the Universe.

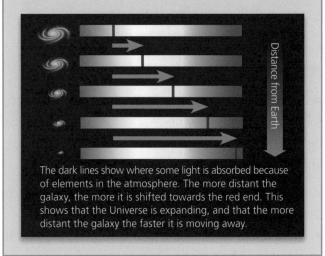

Distance from Earth

The dark lines show where some light is absorbed because of elements in the atmosphere. The more distant the galaxy, the more it is shifted towards the red end. This shows that the Universe is expanding, and that the more distant the galaxy the faster it is moving away.

HT The History of a Star

Stars, including our Sun, are formed when interstellar (between stars) gas clouds, which contain mainly hydrogen, collapse under gravitational attraction to form a **protostar**. Over a very long period of time, the temperature of the protostar increases as thermonuclear fusion reactions take place, releasing massive amounts of energy, and it finally becomes a **main sequence star** for the majority of its life (like our Sun). During this time, the forces of attraction pulling inwards are balanced by forces acting outwards and the star experiences a normal life. Eventually the supply of hydrogen runs out, causing the death of the star. The type of death depends largely on the star's mass.

The End of a Star

All stars have a finite (limited) life. They start as a huge gas cloud that joins up to form a star – all stars have different sizes. Eventually, the star's supply of fusion fuel runs out and the star swells up, becoming colder and colder to form a **red giant** or **red supergiant**.

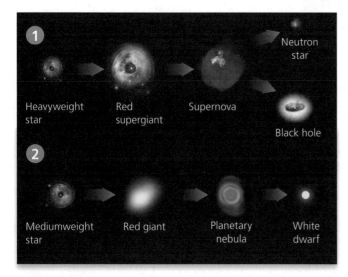

1 Heavyweight star → Red supergiant → Supernova → Neutron star / Black hole

2 Mediumweight star → Red giant → Planetary nebula → White dwarf

1 Death of a Heavyweight Star

Red supergiant to Supernova – when a red supergiant shrinks rapidly and explodes it becomes a supernova, releasing massive amounts of energy, dust and gas into space.

Supernova to Neutron star – for stars up to ten times the mass of our Sun, the remnants of the supernova form a neutron star, which is formed only of neutrons. A cupful of this matter could have a mass greater than 15 000 million tonnes!

Supernova to Black hole – those stars greater than ten times the mass of our Sun are massive enough to leave behind black holes. Black holes can only be observed indirectly through their effects on their surroundings, e.g. the X-rays emitted when gases from a nearby star spiral into a black hole. Not even light can escape from a black hole.

2 Death of a Mediumweight Star

Red giant to Planetary nebula – For a red giant the core contracts and is surrounded by outer layers (shells) of gas which eventually drift away into space.

Planetary nebula to White dwarf – As the core cools and contracts further, it becomes a white dwarf with a density thousands of times greater than any matter on Earth.

> **HT** Black holes can be found throughout the Universe and in every galaxy. They have a very large mass concentrated into a very small space, which means that their gravity is very large. Not even light can escape from black holes.
>
> Black holes are formed at the end of the life of a heavyweight star.

The History of the Universe

We now know that the Earth orbits the Sun. However, in ancient Greece and ancient China, people believed that the Earth was the centre of the Universe and all the planets orbited around it. All the stars seemed to orbit the Pole Star, while those near the Equator would rise and set. They could not imagine that the Earth was moving.

Nicolas Copernicus in Poland was the first person to publish a book (in 1543) which claimed that the Earth and all the other planets orbited the Sun. This was not accepted because it contradicted the religious view in Europe of how the Christian God made the world.

Galileo Galilei in 1610 used the telescope that he had invented to see that Venus had 'phases' like the Moon. This convinced him that the Earth and other planets orbited the Sun, as Copernicus had said.

> **HT** Copernicus and Galileo contradicted the Roman Catholic Church's view of how the Universe was formed. At this time all the philosophers and astronomers believed in the geocentric view with the Sun orbiting the Earth. The Catholic Church described the heliocentric universe (with the planets orbiting the Sun) as 'false and contrary to scripture'. Galileo was tried and convicted of heresy. This made the heliocentric view very unpopular for many years.

1 This question is about a bicycle dynamo.

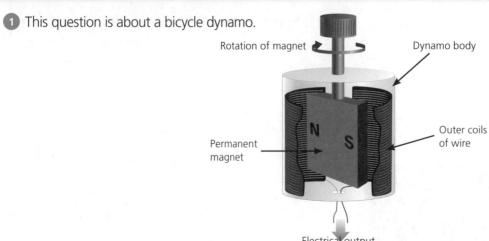

Rotation of magnet

Dynamo body

Permanent magnet

N   S

Outer coils of wire

Electrical output

a) A bicycle dynamo may be used to generate electricity, for example to run a light.
Explain how the electricity is generated. **[2]**

b) A cyclist put in 100J of energy, however only 25J was transferred into electrical energy.
Calculate the efficiency. **[2]**

2 a) Homer Simpson works for a nuclear power plant in Springfield. He has to work with radioactive materials on a regular basis.

There are three different types of nuclear radiation; one of these is alpha radiation. Tick (✓) the other two from the list. **[2]**

Beta radiation ☐   Microwaves ☐   Gamma waves ☐   Radio waves ☐

b) Radioactive materials need to be handled with care.

What safety precautions would you recommend Homer to take? **[2]**

3 Two famous models of the Universe are the Ptolemaic model and the Copernican model.
Describe the similarities and differences between these two models. **[6]**

The quality of written communication will be assessed in your answer to this question.

HT 4 Figures show that our atmosphere is warming up. One suggestion as to why this is happening is the greenhouse effect.

a) Explain how the greenhouse effect works. **[3]**

b) Some researchers investigate where warming of the atmosphere is greatest. One location they have found is near to a factory. Suggest why there could be greater warming here. **[2]**

c) One way to reduce our emissions of greenhouse gases is to look into 'greener' fuels, for example wind power. Wind power is a renewable source and it doesn't produce polluting waste. However, it has a few disadvantages. Describe two of these disadvantages. **[2]**

d) Although the greenhouse effect theory is widely accepted, some scientists disagree with it.
Argue for and against this theory. **[6]**
The quality of written communication will be assessed in your answer to this question.

P3: Forces for Transport

This module looks at:

- Speed, distance and time, alongside transport and road safety.
- Acceleration and how to measure it.
- Thinking, braking and stopping distances when driving.
- Work done, power and energy in relation to car use.
- Transport and energy, including the use of fossil fuels and the use of biofuels and solar power.
- How energy is absorbed during collisions, and car safety features.
- Falling objects and the balance of forces.
- Theme park rides and their forces and energy, including gravity and potential energy and kinetic energy.

Speed

One way to describe the movement of an object is by measuring its **speed**, i.e. how fast it is moving.

A faster object will travel a longer distance in a given time. Or a faster object will take less time to travel a certain distance.

Speed is measured in:

- **metres per second (m/s)**
- **kilometres per hour (km/h)**
- **miles per hour (mph).**

For example, the cyclist in the diagram below travels a distance of 8 metres every second, so his speed is 8m/s.

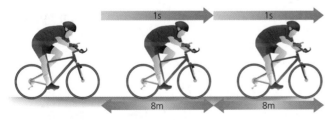

To work out the speed of any moving object two things must be known:

- the **distance** it travels (which can be measured

using a measuring tape or a trundle wheel)
- the **time taken** to travel that distance (which can be measured using a stopclock).

The speed of an object can be calculated using the equation:

$$\text{Speed (m/s)} = \frac{\text{Distance travelled (m)}}{\text{Time taken (s)}}$$

where v is speed

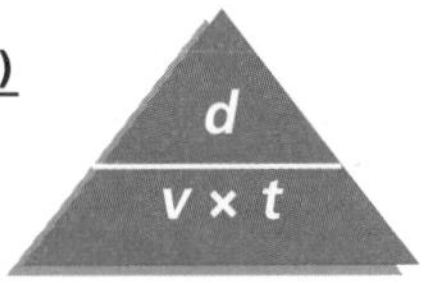

$$\frac{d}{v \times t}$$

The faster the speed of an object, the shorter the time it takes to travel a particular distance.

Example 1

Calculate the speed of a cyclist who travels 2400m in 5 minutes. Use the formula:

$$\text{Speed} = \frac{\text{Distance}}{\text{Time taken}}$$

$$= \frac{2400\text{m}}{300\text{s}} = \textbf{8m/s}$$

You need to be able to rearrange the speed formula in order to calculate either distance or time taken.

Example 2

A car is travelling at a constant speed of 80km/h. Calculate the distance it travels in 90 minutes. Rearrange the formula:

$$\text{Distance} = \text{Speed} \times \text{Time taken}$$
$$= 80\text{km/h} \times 1.5\text{h} = \textbf{120km}$$

Example 3

Calculate the time it takes a motorcyclist to travel a distance of 120km at 50km/h. Rearrange the formula:

$$\text{Time taken} = \frac{\text{Distance}}{\text{Speed}}$$

$$= \frac{120\text{km}}{50\text{km/h}} = 2.4\text{h} = \textbf{2h 24min}$$

Distance and Average Speed

For an object that is changing speed (uniformly) it is possible to calculate the distance it travels by using the average speed:

$$\text{Distance} = \text{Average speed} \times \text{Time}$$

$$\text{Distance} = \frac{(u + v)}{2} \times t$$

where u is the starting speed and v is the final speed

Distance and Average Speed (cont)

Example

A bike travelling at 2 m/s increases in speed to 10 m/s in 20 seconds. How far does it travel in this time?

$$\text{Distance} = \text{Average speed} \times \text{Time}$$
$$= \frac{(10 + 2)}{2} \times 20$$
$$= 6 \times 20 = \textbf{120m}$$

Speed Cameras

Speed cameras take two pictures of a vehicle, one a certain amount of time after the other. The position of the vehicle in relation to the distance markings on the road in the two pictures are used to calculate the speed of the vehicle, using the following formula:

$$\text{Speed of car} = \frac{\text{Distance travelled between pictures}}{\text{Time between first and second picture}}$$

Average-speed cameras are often used on motorways. A camera takes a photo of the car number plate and a second camera takes a photo of the same car later. The time between the photos and the distance between the cameras is used to work out the average speed.

Distance–Time Graphs

The slope of a **distance–time graph** represents the speed of an object: the steeper the slope, the faster the speed. The y-axis shows the distance from a fixed point (0, 0), not the total distance travelled.

If an object (e.g. a person) is standing 10m from point (0, 0) and is not moving, the distance–time graph would look like this:

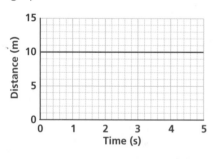

$$\frac{10 - 10}{5} = 0\text{m/s}$$

If the person starts at point (0, 0) and moves at a constant speed of 2m/s, the graph would look like this:

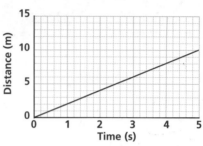

$$\frac{10 - 0}{5} = 2\text{m/s}$$

If the person starts at point (0, 0) and moves at a greater constant speed of 3m/s, the graph would look like this:

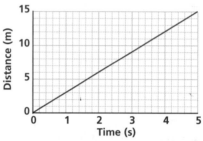

$$\frac{15 - 0}{5} = 3\text{m/s}$$

The speed of an object can be calculated by working out the gradient of a distance–time graph: the steeper the gradient, the faster the speed. Take any point on the graph and read off the distance travelled for that part of the journey and the time taken to get there. Use this to work out the speed.

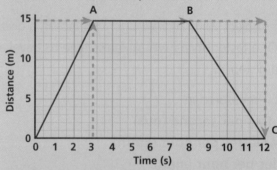

So, the object travelled at 5m/s for 3 seconds, remained stationary for 5 seconds then travelled backwards at 3.75m/s for 4 seconds until it reached the starting point.

Distance–Time Graphs for Non-Uniform Speed

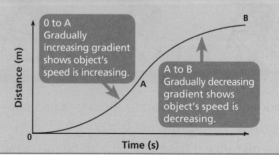

0 to A
Gradually increasing gradient shows object's speed is increasing.

A to B
Gradually decreasing gradient shows object's speed is decreasing.

Speed–Time Graphs

A speed–time graph plots a person's or object's speed at different times.

The slope of a **speed–time graph** represents the acceleration of an object.

A constant acceleration gradually increases the speed at a uniform rate. The steeper the slope (from bottom left to top right), the bigger the acceleration.

A negative gradient slope (from top left to bottom right) indicates **deceleration** (decreasing speed).

1 **Constant Speed**

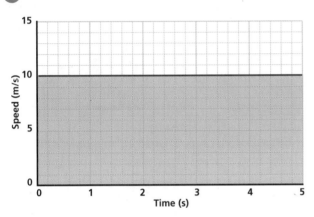

Object is moving at a constant speed of 10m/s, i.e. it is not accelerating.

$$\frac{10 - 10}{5} = 0\text{m/s}^2$$

2 **Increasing Speed**

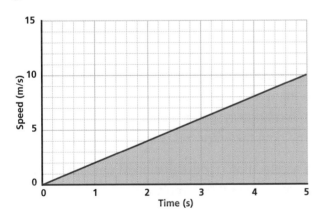

Object's constant acceleration is 2m/s².

$$\frac{10 - 0}{5} = 2\text{m/s}^2$$

3 **Increasing Speed**

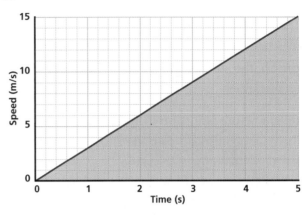

Object's constant acceleration is 3m/s².

$$\frac{15 - 0}{5} = 3\text{m/s}^2$$

4 **Decreasing Speed**

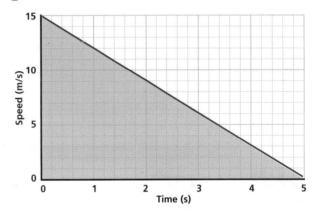

Object's constant acceleration is -3m/s².

$$\frac{0 - 15}{5} = -3\text{m/s}^2$$

HT The area underneath the line in a speed–time graph represents the total distance travelled.

For example, the area under the line in graph **3** ($\frac{1}{2} \times 15 \times 5 = 37.5$m) is greater than the area under the line in graph **2** ($\frac{1}{2} \times 10 \times 5 = 25$m).

This means that the distance travelled by the object in graph **3** is greater than the distance travelled by the object in graph **2** for the same time period.

ⓗ Speed–Time Graphs (cont)

The **acceleration** of an object can be calculated by working out the **gradient** of a **speed–time graph**: the steeper the gradient, the bigger the acceleration.

Take any two points on the graph and read off the change in speed over the chosen period, and the time taken for this change.

So, the object accelerated at 5m/s² for 3 seconds, then travelled at a constant speed of 15m/s for 5 seconds (zero acceleration), and then decelerated at a rate of 3.75m/s² for 4 seconds.

Distance travelled = Area of 0AX + Area of ABYX + Area of BCY
$= (\frac{1}{2} \times 3 \times 15) + (5 \times 15) + (\frac{1}{2} \times 4 \times 15) = $ **127.5m**

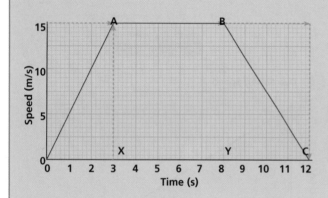

Speed–Time Graph for Non-Uniform Motion

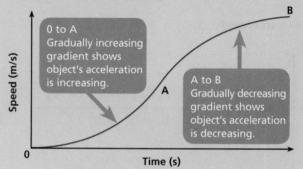

0 to A
Gradually increasing gradient shows object's acceleration is increasing.

A to B
Gradually decreasing gradient shows object's acceleration is decreasing.

Acceleration

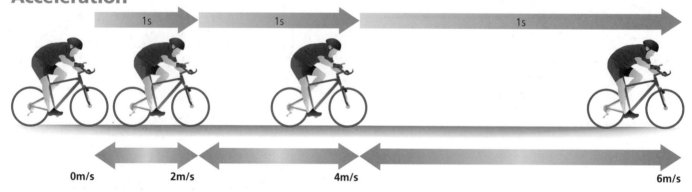

0m/s   2m/s   4m/s   6m/s

The **acceleration** of an object is the **change in speed per second**. In other words, it is a measure of how quickly an object speeds up or slows down.

Acceleration has the unit **metres per second per second (m/s²)**. Since the cyclist in the illustration above increases his speed by 2 metres per second every second, we can say that his acceleration is 2m/s² (2 metres per second, per second).

Acceleration is speeding up. **Deceleration** is slowing down (also called negative acceleration). A greater change in speed in a given time means a bigger acceleration.

To work out the acceleration of any moving object two things must be known:
- the change in speed
- the time taken for this change in speed.

The acceleration or deceleration of an object can be calculated using the formula:

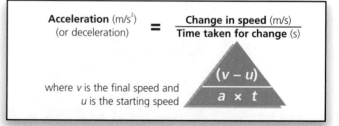

$$\text{Acceleration (m/s}^2\text{)} = \frac{\text{Change in speed (m/s)}}{\text{Time taken for change (s)}}$$
(or deceleration)

where v is the final speed and u is the starting speed

$$\frac{(v-u)}{a \times t}$$

There are two points to be aware of:

- The cyclist in the diagram on page 40 increases his speed by the **same amount** every second, which means the **distance** he travels each second increases.
- Deceleration is simply a negative acceleration, i.e. it describes an object that is slowing down.

Example 1

a) A cyclist accelerates uniformly from rest and reaches a speed of 10m/s after 5 seconds. He then decelerates uniformly and comes to rest in a further 10 seconds. Calculate his acceleration in both cases. Use the formula:

$$a = \frac{(v - u)}{t} \qquad a = \frac{10 - 0 \text{m/s}}{5s} \qquad a = \textbf{2m/s}^2$$

b) Calculate his deceleration. Again, use the formula:

$$a = \frac{(v - u)}{t} \qquad a = \frac{0 - 10 \text{m/s}}{10s} \qquad a = \textbf{-1m/s}^2$$

HT Example 2

An object at rest falls from the top of a building with an acceleration of 10m/s^2. It hits the ground with a speed of 25m/s. Calculate how long the object takes to fall.

Rearrange the formula:

$$\text{Time taken} = \frac{\text{Change in speed}}{\text{Acceleration}}$$
$$= \frac{25 \text{m/s} - 0}{10 \text{m/s}^2} = \textbf{2.5s}$$

Example 3

A car accelerates at 1.5m/s^2 for 12 seconds. If the initial speed of the car was 10m/s, calculate the speed of the car after the acceleration.

Rearrange the formula:

Change in speed = Acceleration × Time taken
$$= 1.5 \text{m/s}^2 \times 12s$$
$$= \textbf{18m/s}$$

$$\frac{\text{Speed of car}}{\text{after acceleration}} = \frac{\text{Initial}}{\text{speed}} + \frac{\text{Change in}}{\text{speed}}$$
$$= 10 \text{m/s} + 18 \text{m/s} = \textbf{28m/s}$$

Relative Velocity

When two objects move in opposite directions at the same speed, their velocities have the same magnitude but opposite signs.

Relative velocity can be calculated using the formula:

Relative velocity	=	Velocity 1	−	Velocity 2

Example

a) A car travelling at 20m/s is following a car travelling at 15m/s. What is the relative velocity of the first car?

Relative velocity = Velocity 1 – Velocity 2
$$= 20 - 15$$
$$= \textbf{5m/s}$$

b) If the cars are travelling in the opposite directions, what is the relative velocity of the cars?

Relative velocity = Velocity 1 – Velocity 2
$$= 20 - -15$$
$$= \textbf{35m/s}$$

Remember:

- Negative acceleration is **deceleration**.
- Negative speed means going in the opposite direction.
- If we need to note the direction an object is moving in we use **velocity**.
- **Velocity** includes information about speed and direction – velocity is speed in a given direction.

HT *N.B. Acceleration can also involve a change of direction and/or speed. It is a vector quantity.*

Acceleration is caused by a force. If the force acts in a different direction to that in which the object is moving – say from the side by the wind – then the object will change direction and experience an acceleration.

Forces in Action

Forces are **pushes** or **pulls**. They are measured in **newtons (N)** and may be different in size and act in different directions. Forces can cause objects to speed up or slow down, for example:

- **gravity** causes an apple falling from a tree to speed up as it falls; it accelerates
- **friction** causes a car to slow down; it decelerates
- **air resistance** causes a parachutist to slow down after opening a parachute; she decelerates.

When the air resistance on the parachute exactly cancels out the downward force of gravity, the parachute will stay at the same speed as it falls. It does not speed up or slow down because the forces are balanced.

The relationship between force, mass and acceleration is shown in the formula:

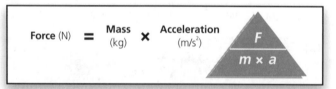

From this formula, we can define a newton (N) as the force needed to give a mass of one kilogram an acceleration of one metre per second per second ($1m/s^2$).

A bigger force on a given mass will cause a bigger acceleration.

Example

A trolley of mass 400kg is accelerating at $0.5m/s^2$. What force is needed to achieve this acceleration?

Use the formula:

$$\text{Force} = \text{Mass} \times \text{Acceleration}$$
$$= 400kg \times 0.5m/s^2$$
$$\mathbf{= 200N}$$

The girl in the diagram below is standing on the ground. She is being pulled down to the ground by gravity, and the ground is pushing up with an equal force – the reaction force.

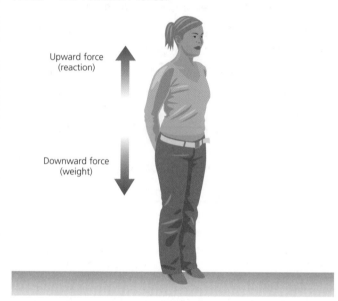

Upward force (reaction)

Downward force (weight)

Stopping Distance

The **stopping distance** of a vehicle depends on:
- the **thinking distance** – the distance travelled by the vehicle from the point the driver realises he needs to brake to when he applies the brakes
- the **braking distance** – the distance travelled by the vehicle from the point the driver applies the brakes to the point at which the vehicle actually stops.

Stopping distance = Thinking distance + Braking distance

The **thinking distance** is increased if:
- the vehicle is travelling faster
- the driver is ill, tired or under the influence of alcohol or drugs
- the driver is distracted or is not fully concentrating
- there is poor visibility – this delays the time before the driver realises he needs to apply the brakes.

Stopping Distance (cont)

The **braking distance** is increased if:

- the vehicle is travelling faster
- there are poor weather or road conditions, e.g. if it is wet, slippery or icy
- the vehicle is in poor condition, e.g. brakes and tyres are worn out, tyres are not inflated properly.

A longer thinking distance and a longer braking distance means the car takes longer to stop (longer stopping distance).

Drivers should not drive too close to the car in front and should always keep to the speed limit (or below if road or driving conditions are poor) so that the stopping distance is long enough to avoid an accident.

The illustration below shows how the thinking distance and braking distance of a vehicle under normal driving conditions depend on the vehicle's speed.

It takes much longer to stop at faster speeds, which is why, for safety, drivers should always:

- obey the speed limits
- keep their distance from the car in front (more than the stopping distance)
- allow extra room between cars, or drive more slowly in bad weather or poor road conditions.

HT As the speed of a car increases:

- the driver's thinking distance increases linearly
- the driver's braking distance increases as the square of the speed:
  - speed doubles, braking distance increases by a factor of 4
  - speed trebles, braking distance increases by a factor of 9.

The braking distance of a vehicle is increased if:

- the **mass** of the vehicle is **increased** – a loaded vehicle, i.e. a vehicle with passengers, baggage etc. has a higher kinetic energy, which increases the braking distance
- the **friction** between the tyres and the road is **decreased** – a wet or greasy road surface reduces the amount of friction between the tyres and the road, which increases the braking distance
- the **braking force** applied is **decreased** – a smaller force exerted by the brake pads on the wheel discs increases the braking distance
- the vehicle is **travelling faster** – a faster vehicle has higher kinetic energy, which increases the braking distance.

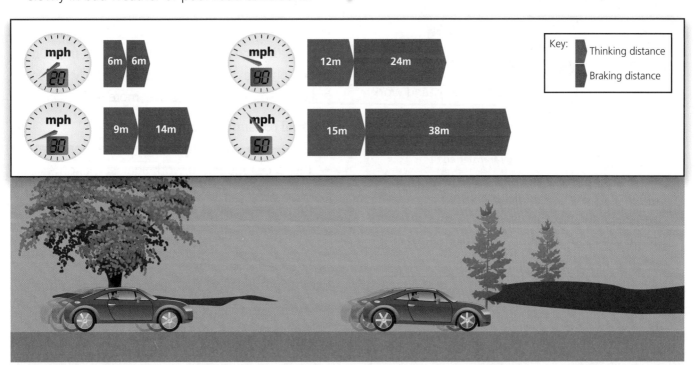

Work

Work is done whenever a force moves an object. Every day you are doing work and developing **power**, for example in activities like:

- lifting weights
- climbing stairs
- pulling a wheelie bin
- pushing a shopping trolley.

Energy is needed to do work. Both energy and work are measured in **joules, J**:

> **Work done** (J) **= Energy transferred** (J)

The amount of work done depends on:

- the **size** of the force in newtons
- the **distance** the object is moved in metres in the direction of the force.

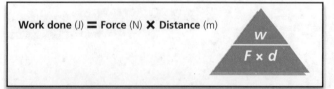

> **Work done** (J) **= Force** (N) **× Distance** (m)
>
> $$\frac{W}{F \times d}$$

Example

A man pushes a car with a steady force of 250N. The car moves a distance of 20m. How much work does the man do?

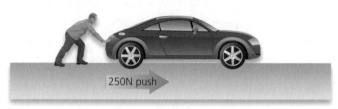

250N push

$$
\begin{aligned}
\text{Work done} &= \text{Force} \times \text{Distance} \\
&= 250\text{N} \times 20\text{m} \\
&= \textbf{5000J (or 5kJ)}
\end{aligned}
$$

Weight

If you are lifting your own weight, you are doing work.

> **Weight** (N) **= Mass** (kg) **× Gravitational field strength** (N/kg)

Example

A person has a mass of 60kg. Calculate their weight on Earth where the gravitational field strength is 10N/kg. Use the equation:

$$
\begin{aligned}
\text{Weight} &= \text{Mass} \times \text{Gravitational field strength} \\
&= 60\text{kg} \times 10\text{N/kg} \\
&= \textbf{600N}
\end{aligned}
$$

Fuel Consumption

Different cars have different power ratings (usually expressed as the number of seconds to get from 0mph to 60mph) and different engine sizes (usually expressed as litres – so a larger engine uses more fuel).

Car **fuel consumption** depends on:

- the engine size – larger engines use more fuel
- the force required to work against friction
- driving style and speed – more accelerating and braking uses more fuel
- road conditions
- tyre pressure.

Obviously, using more fuel has a bigger impact on the environment – using more resources, creating more pollutants in the exhaust gases and costing more money.

Power

Power is a measure of how quickly work is done, i.e. the work done per second. The unit of power is the **watt, W**.

Some cars have much higher **power ratings** than others and they may also use far more fuel. High fuel consumption is expensive for the driver and is also damaging to the environment.

Power, work done and time taken are linked by the formula:

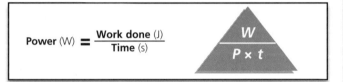

$$\text{Power (W)} = \frac{\text{Work done (J)}}{\text{Time (s)}} \qquad \frac{W}{P \times t}$$

Example 1

A girl of mass 60kg runs up a flight of stairs to a height of 4m in 8 seconds. What is her power?

$$\text{Weight of girl} = \text{Mass} \times \text{Gravitational field strength}$$
$$W = 60\text{kg} \times 10\text{N/kg}$$
$$= \mathbf{600N}$$

Work done running up stairs:
$$\text{Work done} = \text{Force} \times \text{Distance}$$
$$= 600\text{N} \times 4\text{m}$$
$$= \mathbf{2400J}$$

So the girl does 2400 joules of work when she runs up a flight of stairs in 8 seconds. Calculate her power.

$$\text{Power} = \frac{\text{Work done}}{\text{Time}}$$
$$= \frac{2400\text{J}}{8\text{s}}$$
$$= \mathbf{300W}$$

HT ### Example 2

A crane does 200 000J of work when it lifts a load of 25 000N. The power of the crane is 50kW.

a) Calculate the distance moved by the load.
   Rearrange the formula:
$$\text{Distance} = \frac{\text{Work done}}{\text{Force}}$$
$$= \frac{200\ 000\text{J}}{25\ 000\text{N}}$$
$$= \mathbf{8m}$$

b) Calculate the time taken to move the load.
   Rearrange the formula:
$$\text{Time} = \frac{\text{Work done}}{\text{Power}}$$
$$= \frac{200\ 000\text{J}}{50\ 000\text{W}}$$
$$= \mathbf{4s}$$

Power can also be calculated using **Force × Speed**.

This comes from:
$$\text{Power} = \frac{\text{Work done}}{\text{Time}}, \text{ and}$$
$$\text{Work done} = \text{Force} \times \text{Distance}$$
$$\text{Therefore,} \quad \text{Power} = \text{Force} \times \frac{\text{Distance}}{\text{Time}}$$
$$\text{Thus,} \quad \text{Power} = \text{Force} \times \text{Speed}$$

$$\frac{P}{F \mid S}$$

Kinetic Energy

Kinetic energy is the energy an object has because of its movement, i.e. if it is moving it has got kinetic energy. Kinetic energy is measured in joules.

The following all have kinetic energy:
- a ball rolling along the ground
- a car travelling along a road
- a person running.

Kinetic energy depends on two things:
- the **mass** of the object (kg)
- the **speed** of the object (m/s).

A moving car has kinetic energy because it has both mass and speed. If the car moves with a faster speed it has more kinetic energy (providing its mass has not changed).

> **HT** If the mass of the car is greater (e.g. there are more people inside it, or it is a larger vehicle, e.g. a truck), it may have more kinetic energy even if its speed is less than that of another car.
>
> A car with more kinetic energy will have a longer braking distance because there is more energy to get rid of using the brakes (which is why they get hot).

You can calculate kinetic energy using the formula:

$$\text{Kinetic energy (J)} = \frac{1}{2} \times \text{Mass (kg)} \times \text{Speed}^2 \text{ (m/s)}^2$$

Example 1

A car of mass 1000kg is moving at a speed of 10m/s. How much kinetic energy does it have?

Use the formula:
$$\text{Kinetic energy} = \frac{1}{2} \times \text{Mass} \times \text{Speed}^2$$
$$= \frac{1}{2} \times 1000\text{kg} \times (10\text{m/s})^2$$
$$= \textbf{50 000J (or 50kJ)}$$

Example 2

Calculate the kinetic energy of a toy car of mass 400g moving at a speed of 0.5m/s. Use the formula:
$$\text{Kinetic energy} = \frac{1}{2} \times \text{Mass} \times \text{Speed}^2$$
$$= \frac{1}{2} \times 0.4\text{kg} \times (0.5\text{m/s})^2$$
$$= \textbf{0.05J}$$

Fuels

Although most cars rely on **fossil fuels** such as **petrol** or **diesel** for their energy, it is also possible to use **biodiesel**. Biodiesel is a liquid fuel made from plants. The main disadvantage is that these plants are grown in fields that could have been used to grow other plants for food.

Electricity can also be used. **Battery-driven** cars are already on our roads and **solar-powered** cars with solar panels on their roofs will soon follow. Solar-powered cars would produce no pollution. Unlike cars powered by fossil fuels, cars powered by electricity do not pollute at the point of use. However, their batteries are recharged using electricity that is generated in power stations, which does cause pollution.

There may be an overall reduction in carbon dioxide production to generate this energy when power stations are better set up to control pollution and emissions. However, in the UK we do not have enough power stations to produce enough electricity if everyone had electric cars and the National Grid could not transmit enough current to charge all the batteries.

Our supplies of fossil fuels are running low and pollution and **climate change** are now such big problems that cars will soon have to run on less polluting fuels such as biofuels, electricity or **hydrogen fuel cells**.

> **HT** Biofuels use fuel from crops so the carbon dioxide emitted is balanced by the carbon dioxide taken in by the crops when they were growing.
>
> However, producing biofuels and transporting them to users requires conventional fossil fuels. This means that pollution is produced in production, even if there is less pollution produced at the point of use.
>
> Solar-powered vehicles do not pollute because they generate electricity from the Sun.
>
> However, they are unreliable in the UK because there is so little sunlight. Producing solar panels does produce pollution and uses up valuable resources, so they are not completely pollution-free.

Vehicle Fuel Consumption

Designing better vehicle shapes can reduce their air resistance, which improves their fuel consumption as well as giving them higher top speeds, for example:

- sports cars are wedge shaped
- lorries and caravans often have deflectors on top to given them a less 'boxy' shape.

Fuel consumption is increased by increased air resistance, such as roof boxes on top of cars and driving with the windows down.

> **HT** Car **fuel consumption** depends on:
> - the energy required to increase kinetic energy
> - the energy required to work against friction
> - driving style and speed – more accelerating and braking uses more fuel
> - different road conditions
> - tyre pressure.

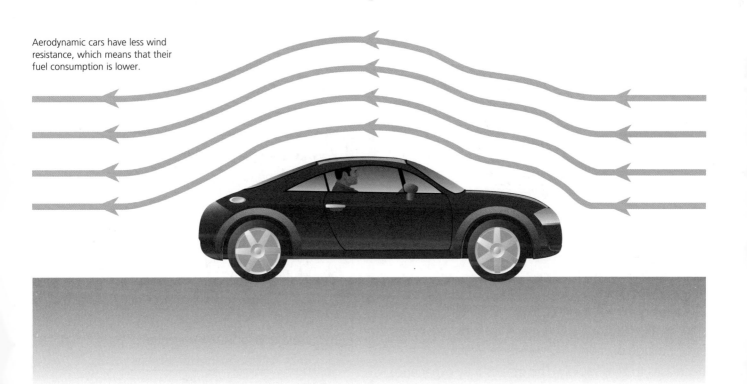

Aerodynamic cars have less wind resistance, which means that their fuel consumption is lower.

Momentum

Momentum is calculated using:

$$\underset{\text{(kg m/s)}}{\text{Momentum}} = \underset{\text{(kg)}}{\text{Mass}} \times \underset{\text{(m/s)}}{\text{Velocity}}$$

So if a vehicle has more mass or is travelling faster it has more momentum.

Example 1
Calculate the momentum of a bullet of mass 10g travelling at 300m/s.

Momentum = Mass × Velocity

= 0.01kg × 300m/s = **3 kg m/s**

Example 2
If a ball of mass 300g has a momentum the same as the bullet above, how fast is it travelling?

$$\text{Velocity} = \frac{\text{Momentum}}{\text{Mass}}$$

$$\text{Velocity} = \frac{3\text{kg m/s}}{0.3\text{kg}} = \textbf{10 m/s}$$

Force

Force can be calculated using:

$$\underset{\text{(N)}}{\text{Force}} = \frac{\text{Change of momentum (kg m/s)}}{\text{Time (s)}}$$

Example
In example 1 above, if the bullet is shot from the gun and accelerates to its full speed in 0.01 seconds then what is the force on it? The bullet's momentum goes from 0 to 3 kg m/s in 0.01 seconds.

$$\text{Force} = \frac{\text{Momentum change}}{\text{Time}}$$

$$= \frac{3 - 0}{0.01} = \textbf{300N}$$

Car Safety Features

In a car accident the driver and passengers decelerate very quickly and therefore experience a large change of momentum as their velocity decreases to zero rapidly. This means they experience a very large force, which can cause injuries.

Modern cars have **safety features** that **absorb energy** during a collision, thereby reducing the injuries. These safety features include:

- **seat belts** – that stretch slightly and also have a mechanism in the base which means the person's energy is absorbed
- **air bags** – to cushion the impact for the driver and front passenger
- **brakes** – to reduce the speed of the car by transferring kinetic energy to heat energy
- **crumple zone** – a region of the car designed specifically to 'crumple' during a collision. This absorbs a lot of the energy in a crash, reducing the danger to the people in the car.

Crumple zones, seat belts and air bags all **change shape** on impact to **absorb energy** and therefore reduce the risk of injury to the people in the car. They also lengthen the time that the passenger takes to stop. This means that a passenger's momentum changes over a longer time so they experience less force and suffer fewer injuries.

Seat belts have to be replaced after a crash because they can be damaged (perhaps stretched) by the force of a body against them. The benefit of seat belts is the potential to reduce injury. There is a very slight risk that a passenger might be trapped in a car by their seat belt after an accident and not be able to get out. On balance though, it is always better to wear a seat belt.

HT Newton's second law of motion, often written as $F = ma$ can explain why force is calculated as change of momentum divided by time.

Force = Mass × Acceleration, and

$$\text{Acceleration} = \frac{\text{Change in velocity}}{\text{Time}}$$

$$\text{So, Force} = \text{Mass} \times \frac{\text{Change in velocity}}{\text{Time}}$$

$$\text{Or, Force} = \frac{\text{Mass} \times \text{Change in velocity}}{\text{Time}}$$

But, Mass × Velocity = Momentum

$$\text{So, Force} = \frac{\text{Change in momentum}}{\text{Time}}$$

Safety Features to Prevent Accidents

Some safety features on a car are there to **prevent accidents** (passive safety features). For example:

- **Anti-lock braking systems** (ABS) – prevent the tyres from skidding, which means the vehicle stops more quickly and allows the driver to remain in control of the steering.
- **Traction control** – prevents the car from skidding when accelerating, so the driver can quickly escape from a dangerous situation.
- **Electric windows** – make it easier for the driver to open or close the windows when driving, causing less of a distraction.
- **Paddle shift controls** – allow the driver to keep both hands on the steering wheel when changing gear and adjusting the radio.

Safety Features to Protect Passengers

Some safety features **protect the car's occupants** (active safety features). For example:

- **Crumple zones** – the car bonnet crumples absorbing energy making the passengers slow down more gently.
- **Collapsible steering columns** – so that the driver isn't injured when he/she hits the steering wheel in an accident.
- **Airbags** – protect passengers by inflating to provide a cushioning effect to absorb energy instead of the passengers hitting the dashboard.
- **Seat belts** – hold the passengers in place so that they are not flung through the windscreen on impact.
- **Safety cage** – a metal cage which strengthens the cabin section of the car to prevent the vehicle from collapsing when it is upside down or rolling.

Safety Cage Reinforces Body of Car

HT Wearing a seat belt is compulsory in the UK in both the front and back seats (if seat belts are fitted). This law was brought in to protect people from injuries and to reduce the cost to the National Health Service of treating people after car accidents.

Data from crash tests where dummy drivers and passengers are observed during a controlled crash can identify how the worst injuries happen. This allows car manufacturers to include improved safety features such as side impact bars.

HT Reducing Stopping Forces

The stopping **forces** experienced by the people in the car in a collision can be reduced by:

- increasing the stopping or collision time
- increasing the stopping or collision distance
- decreasing acceleration.

Because force is calculated by **change of momentum divided by time**, this means that the force on a passenger's body is smaller and so the passenger is less likely to be injured badly.

All the safety features mentioned on this page perform one or more of the above tasks. By reducing the stopping forces on the people in the car, they reduce the risk of injury.

Anti-lock braking systems prevent the tyres from skidding during heavy braking by pumping on and off rather than holding the wheel tight. This increases the area of the tyres in contact with the road and gives the driver better control of the car. This often reduces the overall braking distance.

Friction and Air Resistance

Frictional forces, such as **drag**, **friction** and **air resistance**, can act against the movement of an object, slowing it down. They reduce the object's kinetic energy. This effect can be reduced by:

- changing the **shape** (to increase or decrease air resistance)
- using a **lubricant** (to make the object slide with less resistance).

The **shape** of an object can influence its top speed:
- **Shuttlecocks** in badminton are designed to increase air resistance so they travel slower.
- **Parachutes** are designed to have a larger surface area to increase air resistance.
- **Flying squirrels** have skin between their legs and arms to create a large surface area to stop them falling too quickly between tree branches.

Falling objects speed up as they fall because they are pulled towards the centre of the Earth by **gravity**.

Terminal Speed

Falling objects experience two forces:
- the downward force of **weight**, W, which always stays the same on Earth and happens because of the pull of the Earth's gravity
- the upward force of **air resistance**, R, or drag, which increases the faster the object falls.

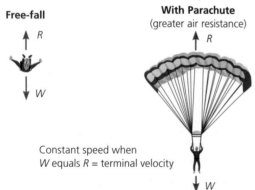

Free-fall

↑ R

↓ W

With Parachute
(greater air resistance)

↑ R

Constant speed when
W equals R = terminal velocity

↓ W

When the weight is bigger than the air resistance then the object speeds up. When the air resistance is bigger than the weight, then the object slows down. If the air resistance is the same as the weight then the forces are balanced and the object continues at the same speed – **its terminal velocity.**

Weight and Gravity

Objects **fall** because of their **weight** and they get faster as they fall. Weight is a **force** pulling towards the centre of a planet – in our case, Earth. The strength of this force depends on the **gravity** of the planet. On the Earth the acceleration caused by gravity is the same on all objects at any particular point on the Earth's surface.

If there is no atmosphere there can be no air resistance (drag). This means that falling objects can not slow down. This happens on the Moon; all objects fall at the same rate on the Moon (nothing can float!).

HT The **Earth's gravitational field strength** (or acceleration due to gravity) is unaffected by atmospheric changes but can be slightly different at different points on the Earth's surface. For example, it will be different at the top of a mountain compared with at the bottom of a mine. But the Earth's field exerts the force required to accelerate the object at exactly the same rate (9.8m/s^2).

HT Drag on an object varies. There is more drag on an object with a larger surface area and on a faster object.

When an object's drag force equals its driving force then the two will balance and the object travels at a constant speed, called the **terminal velocity**.

When a skydiver jumps out of an aeroplane, the speed of his descent can be considered:
- before his parachute opens (i.e. free-fall)
- after his parachute opens (air resistance is increased due to the surface area of his parachute).

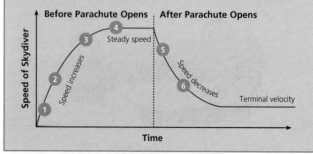

Before Parachute Opens | **After Parachute Opens**

Speed of Skydiver

Speed increases

Steady speed

Speed decreases

Terminal velocity

Time

Gravitational Potential Energy

Gravitational potential energy (GPE) is the energy that an object has due to its position in the Earth's gravitational field. If an object can fall (e.g. a diver standing on a diving board before jumping off) it has gravitational potential energy.

A person standing on a higher diving board will have more gravitational potential energy than another person standing on a lower diving board (providing they have the same mass). This is because he is further away from the ground (see 1).

A heavier person standing on the same diving board as a lighter person will have more gravitational potential energy. This is because he has a bigger mass (see 2).

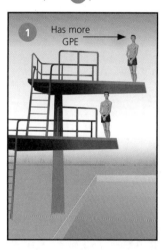

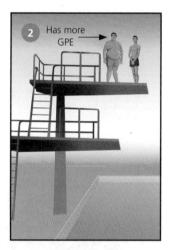

When an object falls it transfers gravitational potential energy into kinetic energy (KE). This is what happens when:

- a diver jumps off the diving board
- a ball rolls down a hill
- a skydiver jumps out of a plane.

An object's KE increases (it gets faster) as its GPE reduces (it gets closer to the ground).

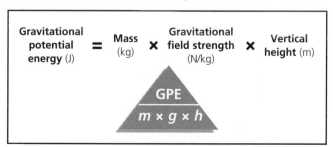

Gravitational potential energy (J) = **Mass** (kg) × **Gravitational field strength** (N/kg) × **Vertical height** (m)

$$\frac{GPE}{m \times g \times h}$$

HT Gravitational field strength, *g*, is a constant. On Earth it has a value of **10N/kg**. This means that every 1kg of matter near the surface of the Earth experiences a downwards force of 10N due to gravity.

On planets where the gravitational field strength is higher, the gravitational potential energy is greater.

Example 1

A skier of mass 80kg gets on a ski lift that takes her from a height of 1000m to a height of 3000m above ground. By how much does her gravitational potential energy increase? Use the formula:

$GPE = m \times g \times h$

$= 80\text{kg} \times 10\text{N/kg} \times (3000\text{m} - 1000\text{m})$

$= 80\text{kg} \times 10\text{N/kg} \times 2000\text{m}$

= 1 600 000J (or 1600kJ)

N.B. Work has been done by the ski-lift motor so that the skier can increase her gravitational potential energy. In other words, work done by the motor has been transferred into her gravitational potential energy. She will transfer this gravitational potential energy into kinetic energy as she skis down the slope.

Example 2

A ball is kicked vertically upwards from the ground. Its mass is 0.2kg and it increases its gravitational potential energy by 30J when it reaches the top point in its flight. What height does the ball reach? Rearrange the formula:

$$\text{Vertical height} = \frac{\text{GPE}}{\text{Mass} \times \text{Gravitational field strength}}$$

$$= \frac{30\text{J}}{0.2\text{kg} \times 10\text{N/kg}}$$

$$= \mathbf{15m}$$

Gravitational Potential Energy and Kinetic Energy

When an object falls, its **gravitational potential energy** is transferred to **kinetic energy**. There are many theme park rides that use this transfer of energy.

1. On most roller-coasters, the cars start high up with a lot of gravitational potential energy.
2. As the cars drop, the gravitational potential energy is gradually transferred into kinetic energy.
3. The car reaches its highest speed, maximum kinetic energy, at the bottom of the slope.
4. As the car climbs the slope on the other side, kinetic energy is converted back into gravitational potential energy, and it slows down.

If the **mass** of the car is **doubled**, the **kinetic energy** also **doubles**.

If the **speed** of the car is **doubled**, the **kinetic energy quadruples**.

Increasing the **gravitational field strength**, will increase the **gravitational potential energy**, but this would require you to move the roller-coaster to a different planet!

HT When an object is falling, the GPE is transferred to KE if it speeds up.

So $mgh = \frac{1}{2}mv^2$

You can work out what height of roller-coaster you need to allow the car to achieve a certain speed.

Example

If you want the car to get up to a speed of 20 m/s at the end of a drop, how high must it start? Assuming that no other work is done:

$$mgh = \frac{1}{2}mv^2$$
$$h = \frac{v^2}{2g}$$
$$h = \frac{20 \times 20}{2 \times 10}$$
$$h = \frac{400}{20} = \mathbf{20m}$$

It is interesting to notice that the mass of the car and occupants makes no difference in this calculation.

When an object is falling at its terminal speed, the speed is not changing, so the kinetic energy does not increase. However, the gravitational potential energy decreases as the object does work against friction or air resistance (gravitational potential energy is transferred into heat and sound energy).

1 Graham makes a journey from home in his car to pick up his friend for lunch. The graph is a distance–time graph of his movements.

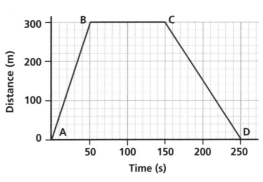

a) Describe Graham's movements at each of the following points: [3]

   i) A to B   ii) B to C   iii) C to D

b) What can you say about his speed on the way there compared to the way back? [1]

c) Calculate Graham's speed during the different parts of the journey. [2]

d) Draw a speed–time graph of his journey. [3]

2 The stopping distance of a car is the combination of the thinking distance and the braking distance.

a) Calculate the stopping distance if the thinking distance is 35m and the braking distance is 45m. [1]

b) Describe two factors for both thinking and stopping distance which would increase their size. [4]

c) If a driver doesn't consider the thinking and braking distance when driving, he/she may be involved in a crash. Most cars are fitted with technology to reduce the effects of a crash and prevent injury, such as crumple zones. Explain how crumple zones work. [3]

3 a) Michelle has just picked up her new car and is driving it home. The mass of her car is 1300kg. She is driving at 50mph (22.3m/s) and enters a 30mph zone, where she slows to 30mph (13.4m/s). Calculate the change in momentum of the car. [2]

b) Whilst driving at 30mph (13.4m/s), Michelle sees a cat run out into the road in front of her and brakes suddenly. The car comes to a stop in 2.2s.

   i) Calculate the change in momentum of the car. [2]

   ii) What force must the brakes apply to stop the car in this time? [3]

HT 4 Eva is on a roller-coaster, as shown in the diagram.

a) Calculate Eva's gravitational potential energy at the top of the peak. She weighs 80kg.
Use gravity as 10N/kg. [2]

b) Eva travels down the slope; all of her gravitational potential energy is converted to kinetic energy. Calculate her speed at the bottom of the slope. [2]

c) After the slope, the roller-coaster stops in 2 seconds. Calculate Eva's deceleration after the slope. [2]

P4: Radiation for Life

This module looks at:

- Medical physics and the importance and problems of electrostatics.
- The uses of electrostatics in medicine and in everyday life.
- Electricity and safety, including earthing and fuses.
- Ultrasound and its medical uses.
- The properties and uses of nuclear radiation.
- The uses of radioisotopes in smoke alarms, cancer treatment, tracers and radioactive dating.
- The properties of waves, including ultrasound.
- Nuclear fission and nuclear fusion, and the use of nuclear fission in producing electricity.

Generating Static Electricity

An **insulating material** can become **electrically charged** if it is rubbed with another insulating material. The charge is called **static electricity** – the electricity stays on the material and does not move. This is due to the **transfer of electrons**.

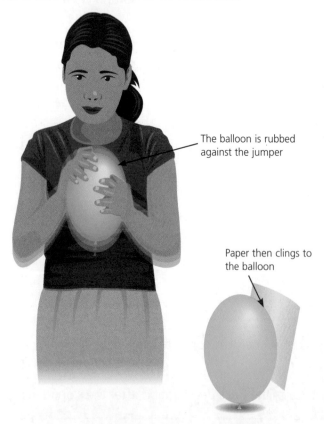

The balloon is rubbed against the jumper

Paper then clings to the balloon

Electrons carry **negative charge**. The electrons transfer from one material to the other, leaving one material with a **positive** charge and the other with a **negative** charge.

You can generate static electricity by rubbing a balloon against a jumper. The electrically charged balloon will then attract light objects, e.g. pieces of paper or cork. The same effect can be obtained using a rubbed comb or strip of plastic. Dusting brushes use this effect. The brushes get charged so that they attract dust when they pass over it, making dusting more effective. Synthetic clothing can become charged up by friction between the clothing and the person's body as they move and this makes the clothing cling. When the clothing is later removed from the body, static sparks are sometimes produced.

Discharging Static Electricity

A charged object can be **discharged** (i.e. have any charge on it removed) by **earthing** it. When an object discharges, electrons are transferred from the charged object to Earth. If you become electrically charged, earthing can result in you getting an **electrostatic shock.**

Touching Water Pipes

A person can become charged up by friction between the soles of their feet and the floor if they are walking on an insulator such as carpet or vinyl. If they then touch a water pipe, e.g. a radiator, the charge is earthed. Discharge occurs, resulting in an electrostatic shock.

Problems of Static Electricity

Some places, such as flour mills and petrochemical factories, have atmospheres that contain extremely flammable gases or high concentrations of fine particles. A discharge of static electricity (i.e. a spark) in these situations can lead to an **explosion**, so factories take precautions to ensure that no spark is made that could ignite the gases.

Static electricity is also dangerous in any situation where large quantities of charge could flow through your body to Earth – lightning, for example. In other situations, static electricity is not dangerous but can be a nuisance, for example:

- it can cause dirt and dust to be attracted to insulators such as television screens and computer monitors
- it can cause some fabrics to cling to your skin.

Repulsion and Attraction

Two insulating materials with the **same charge** will **repel** each other, e.g. two Perspex rods.

For example, if a positively charged rod is held near to a suspended rod which is also positively charged, the suspended rod is repelled. The same effect would happen if both rods had a negative charge.

Two insulating materials with **different charges** will **attract** each other, e.g. a Perspex and an ebonite rod. If a negatively charged rod is held near to a suspended rod which is positively charged, the suspended rod is attracted to it. The same effect would happen if the charges were the other way round.

Repulsion   **Attraction**

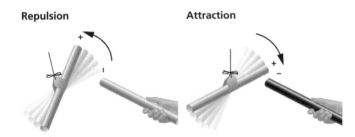

Charging Up Objects

Electric charge (static) builds up when **electrons** (which have a **negative charge**) are rubbed off one material on to another. The material that **receives** the electrons becomes **negatively** charged due to an excess of electrons, while the material **giving up** the electrons becomes **positively** charged due to a loss of electrons.

The atoms or molecules that become charged are then called **ions**.

Example 1

If you rub a Perspex rod with a cloth, the Perspex gives up electrons and becomes positively charged. The cloth receives the electrons and becomes negatively charged.

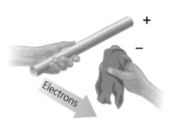

Example 2

If you rub an ebonite rod with fur, the fur gives up some electrons and becomes positively charged. The ebonite receives the electrons and becomes negatively charged.

Reducing the Danger

The chance of receiving an electric shock can be reduced by:

- ensuring that appliances are correctly earthed
- using insulation mats effectively
- wearing shoes with insulating soles.

Lorries that contain flammable gases, liquids or powders need to be earthed before unloading, as friction can cause a build-up of charge. This charge could lead to a spark, which could then ignite the flammable substance.

Anti-static sprays, liquids and cloths help to reduce the problems of static electricity by preventing the transfer of charge from one insulator to another. With no build-up of charge, there can be no discharge.

Connecting an aircraft to a fuel tanker makes sure that any charge built up on the fuel by friction, as it flows through the pipe, flows to Earth, making sure there is no discharge and spark to ignite the fuel.

Using Static in Everyday Life

Defibrillators

Static electricity can be used to start the heart when it has stopped:

- Two paddles are charged and are put in good electrical contact with the patient's chest.
- The defibrillator discharges into the patient.
- Charge is then passed through the patient to make the heart contract.

However, care must be taken not to shock the operator.

Defibrillation

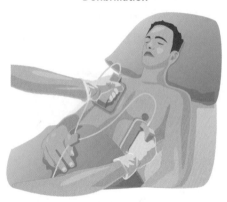

Reducing Smoke Particles in Chimneys

Static electricity is used in electrostatic **dust precipitators** to remove smoke particles from chimneys:

- Metal plates and grids are installed in the chimney and are connected to a high voltage (potential difference). Dust passes through the grid and is charged.
- The dust particles are attracted to earthed plates, where they form larger particles. Large particles fall back down the chimney when they are heavy enough or when the plate is struck.

HT The metal plates in **dust precipitators** are at high voltage. There are also high voltage grids lower down the chimney that make the dust particles charged (they gain or lose electrons). The charged dust particles are attracted to earthed metal plates where they clump together.

Smoke Precipitator

Waste gases

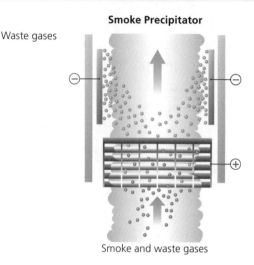

Smoke and waste gases

Spraying

Electrostatics can be useful when spray painting or crop spraying. For example, when spray painting a car:

- The paint gun is negatively charged.
- Paint particles become negatively charged so they repel and spread out evenly.
- The panel that is to be sprayed is made positively charged.
- Paint from the negatively charged paint gun is attracted to the positively charged panel.

HT The negatively charged paint has gained electrons from the gun. The car panel is made positively charged by removing electrons from it to make it attract the paint. This charging process causes the paint to form a fine spray so it is applied evenly. The result is a neutral, painted car panel. It also means that less paint is wasted and even the back and sides of the object that would be in the shadow of the spray receive a coat of paint.

Spray Painting

Negatively charged nozzle

Negatively charged particles of paint

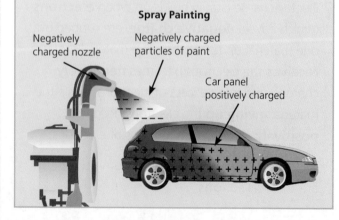

Car panel positively charged

Circuits

A **circuit** is a complete loop that allows an electric current to flow. Electrons flow around the circuit from the negative electrode of the power source to the positive electrode. However, this was only discovered relatively recently so circuit diagrams show the current flowing from the positive electrode to the negative electrode.

Fixed and Variable Resistors

Resistance is a measure of how hard it is to get a **current** through a component in a circuit at a particular **voltage** (potential difference). It is measured in **ohms** (Ω).

The current through a circuit can be controlled by varying the resistance in the circuit. This can be done by using any of the following:

- A **fixed resistor** – a component whose resistance is constant. A higher resistance will give a smaller current for a particular voltage.
  A **longer** piece of resistance wire will give less current for a particular voltage.
  A **thinner** piece of wire will give less current for a particular voltage.
- A **variable resistor** (also known as a **rheostat**) – this component has a resistance that can be altered. A current that flows can be changed by simply moving the sliding contact of the variable resistor from one end to the other, as shown below.

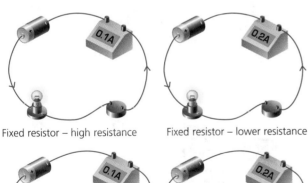

Fixed resistor – high resistance   Fixed resistor – lower resistance

Variable resistor – high resistance   Variable resistor – lower resistance

Current, Voltage and Resistance

Current, voltage and resistance are related by the formula:

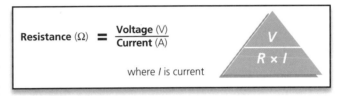

$$\text{Resistance } (\Omega) = \frac{\text{Voltage (V)}}{\text{Current (A)}}$$

where *I* is current

For a **given resistor, current increases as voltage increases** (and vice versa).

For a **fixed voltage, current decreases as resistance increases** (and vice versa).

Example 1
Calculate the resistance of the lamp in the following circuit. Use the formula:

$$\text{Resistance} = \frac{\text{Voltage}}{\text{Current}}$$
$$= \frac{3V}{0.2A}$$
$$= \textbf{15}\,\boldsymbol{\Omega}$$

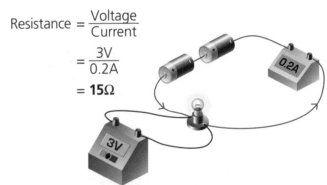

As well as being able to recall the formula above, you should be able to rearrange it to calculate **potential difference** or **current**.

Example 2
Calculate the reading on the ammeter in the circuit below if the bulb has a resistance of 20 ohms.

Rearrange the formula:

$$\text{Current} = \frac{\text{Voltage}}{\text{Resistance}}$$
$$= \frac{6V}{20\Omega}$$
$$= \textbf{0.3A}$$

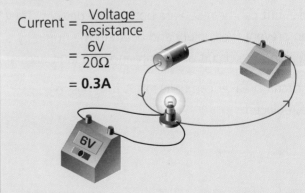

Live, Neutral and Earth Wires

Most electrical appliances are connected to the mains electricity supply using a cable and 3-pin plug, which is inserted into a socket on the ring main circuit. Most cables contain three wires:

- The **live wire** (**brown**) carries current to the appliance at a high voltage – about 230V. (Fuses, circuit breakers and switches are always part of the live wire circuit.)
- The **neutral wire** (**blue**) completes the circuit and carries current away from the appliance.
- The **earth wire** (**green and yellow**) is the safety wire that stops the appliance becoming live.

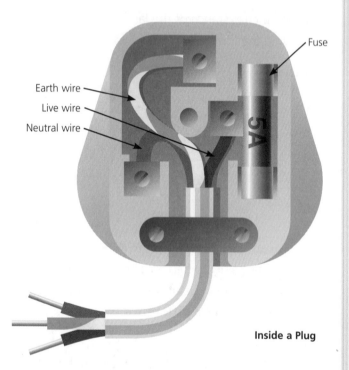

Earth wire
Live wire
Neutral wire
Fuse
5A

Inside a Plug

Fuses and Circuit Breakers

Fuses and **circuit breakers** (devices that act like a fuse, but can be reset) are both safety devices. They can prevent fires, injury and death in the home by breaking the circuit of an appliance if a fault occurs.

A circuit breaker can be reset. A fuse has to be replaced.

How a Fuse Works

A fuse is used to prevent cables or appliances from overheating and/or catching fire.

If a fault causes the current in the appliance to exceed the current rating of the fuse:

- the fuse wire gets hot and melts or breaks
- the circuit is broken so no current can flow
- the fuse prevents the flex/cable overheating
- the appliance is protected.

HT However, for this safety system to work properly, the **current rating** of the fuse must be **just above** the normal current that flows through the appliance.

Insulators wear away and wires touch

As the current increases the fuse gets hotter

The fuse melts and breaks the circuit

Choosing the Right Fuse

The following equation is used to choose the correct fuse:

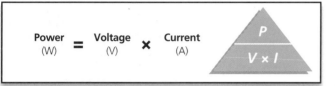

$$\text{Power (W)} = \text{Voltage (V)} \times \text{Current (A)}$$

For example, a computer might have a power rating of 500W. The voltage used in the UK is 230V. Rearranging the formula gives:

$$\text{Current} = \frac{\text{Power}}{\text{Voltage}}$$
$$= \frac{500W}{230V}$$
$$= \textbf{2.2A}$$

So a fuse with a rating just above 2.2A has to be used – a 3 amp fuse would be good.

HT Earthing

All electrical appliances with outer metal cases must have an earth wire to protect the appliance and the user.

This means that the outer case of the appliance is connected to the earth pin in the plug through the earth wire.

This is how it works:
1. A fault in the appliance causes the casing to become live, usually because the live wire touches it.
2. The circuit short-circuits (i.e. the path of the flow of charge changes) because the earth wire offers less resistance. The charge on the metal casing flows along the earth wire as a very large current.
3. The fuse wire melts (or the circuit breaker trips).
4. The circuit is broken.
5. The appliance and the user are protected.

Double Insulation

An earthed conductor cannot become live. This is because earthing means connecting the conductor to Earth, which takes away any charge that could electrocute people.

All appliances with outer metal cases have to be earthed – this means that they have an earth wire.

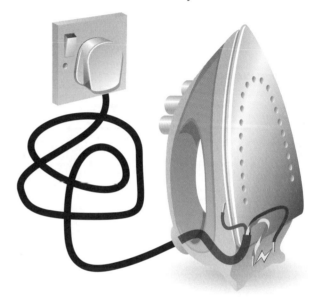

However, the outer cases of some appliances are made of insulators so their cables only need two wires; the earth wire is missing.

These appliances do not need to be earthed because they are **double insulated**; even if the live parts touch the case it does not matter because the case is an insulator.

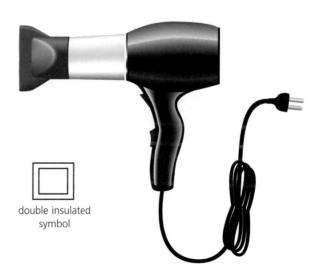

double insulated symbol

Ultrasound

Ultrasound is the name given to sound waves that have frequencies higher than 20 000 hertz (Hz), i.e. above the upper threshold of the human hearing range.

Like all sound waves, ultrasound travels in a **longitudinal** wave. Longitudinal waves can be demonstrated using a slinky spring (see diagram below).

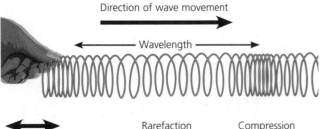

Longitudinal Wave

Direction of wave movement

Wavelength

Hand moves in and out

Rarefaction (loops further apart)

Compression (loops closer together)

The key features of waves are:

- **amplitude** – the maximum disturbance caused by a wave
- **wavelength** – the distance between corresponding points on two successive disturbances, e.g. two compressions
- **frequency** – the number of waves produced (or that pass a particular point) in 1 second.

Applications of Ultrasound

Ultrasound Imaging

Ultrasound can be used in medicine to look inside people, e.g. to scan bodies, measure the speed of blood flow, check that a baby is developing correctly before birth.

Breaking Down Kidney Stones

Ultrasound waves can be used to break down kidney stones in the body so they can be removed without the need for painful surgery.

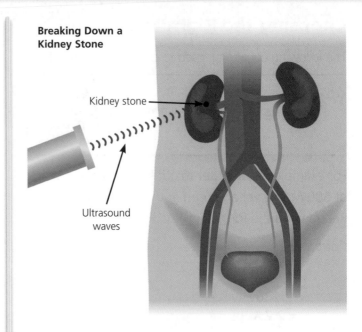

Breaking Down a Kidney Stone

Kidney stone

Ultrasound waves

HT Ultrasonic waves cause the kidney stones to vibrate, making them break up and disperse. They are then passed out of the body in urine.

Body Scans

Ultrasound waves are used to build up a picture of the organs in the body, including the heart, lungs and liver. They can also be used to detect gallstones and tumours. They are used for pre-natal scanning because there is no risk to either the mother or the baby.

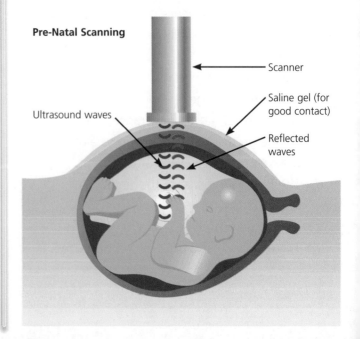

Pre-Natal Scanning

Scanner

Saline gel (for good contact)

Ultrasound waves

Reflected waves

More on Ultrasound

Ultrasound waves are partly reflected at a boundary as they pass from one medium (or substance) into another. The time taken for these reflections to be detected can be used to calculate the depth of the reflecting surface. The reflected waves are usually processed to produce a visual image on a screen.

Ultrasound has two main advantages over X-ray imaging:

- It is able to produce images of soft tissue.
- It does not damage living cells.

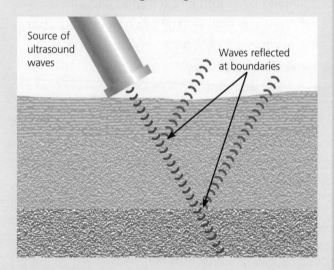

Source of ultrasound waves

Waves reflected at boundaries

Motion of Particles in Waves

All waves **transfer energy** from one point to another **without transferring any particles** of matter. If we allow each coil of a slinky spring to represent one particle, then we can show the movement of the particles in each wave.

Longitudinal Waves

Each particle moves backwards and forwards about its normal position parallel to the direction of wave movement.

Transverse Waves

Each particle moves up and down about its normal position at right angles (90°) to the direction of the wave movement.

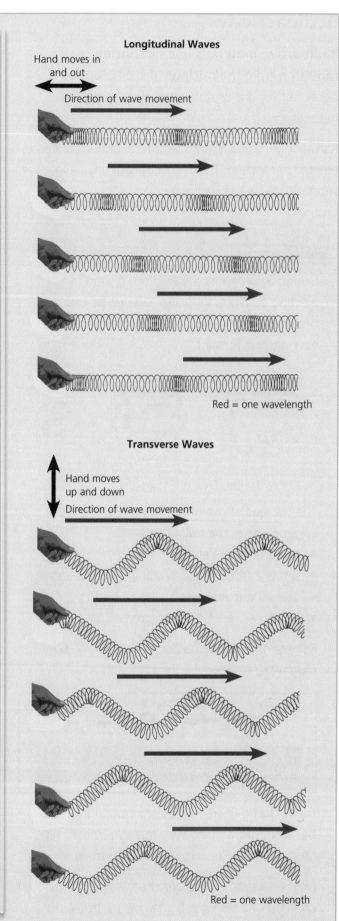

Longitudinal Waves

Hand moves in and out

Direction of wave movement

Red = one wavelength

Transverse Waves

Hand moves up and down

Direction of wave movement

Red = one wavelength

Radioactivity

Radioactive materials give out **nuclear radiation** from the **nucleus** of their atoms because they are unstable and therefore decay naturally.

Radiation is measured by the number of nuclear decays emitted per second. The radioactivity of any radioactive substance decreases with time.

During decay, radiation can be given out in the form of **alpha**, **beta** and **gamma** radiation:

- An alpha particle is like a helium nucleus, i.e. two protons and two neutrons.
- A beta particle is a fast-moving electron.
- A gamma ray is an electromagnetic wave.

When any of this radiation hits an atom it may ionise it. This means it strips off an electron leaving the atom with a positive charge – an **ion**.

Alpha Emission

During alpha emission, an atom decays by ejecting an alpha particle (made up of two protons and two neutrons) from the nucleus. A new atom is formed.

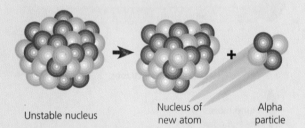

Unstable nucleus   Nucleus of new atom   Alpha particle

The nucleus of the new atom differs from the original one in the following ways:

- It is a different element.
- It has 2 fewer protons and 2 fewer neutrons.
- The atomic number has decreased by 2.
- The mass number has decreased by 4.

For example, the alpha decay of radium-226 into radon-222 is shown by the following equation:

$$^{226}_{88}\text{Ra} \longrightarrow {}^{222}_{86}\text{Rn} + {}^{4}_{2}\alpha$$

The mass numbers (at the top) and the atomic numbers (at the bottom) balance on both sides of the equation.

Alpha particles are particularly good ionisers because they are relatively massive so they hit atoms hard enough to strip off electrons.

N.B. Ionisation means either creating a positively charged or a negatively charged particle (ion).

Beta Emission

During beta emission, an atom decays by changing a neutron into a proton and an electron. The high-energy electron ejected from the nucleus is a beta particle. A new atom is formed by beta decay.

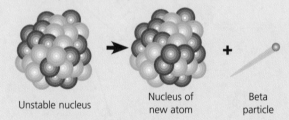

Unstable nucleus   Nucleus of new atom   Beta particle

The nucleus of the new atom differs from the original one in the following ways:

- It is a different element.
- It has 1 more proton and 1 fewer neutron.
- The atomic number has increased by 1.
- The mass number remains the same.

For example, the beta decay of iodine-131 into xenon-131 is shown by the following equation:

$$^{131}_{53}\text{I} \longrightarrow {}^{131}_{54}\text{Xe} + {}^{0}_{-1}\beta$$

Again, the mass numbers and the atomic numbers balance on both sides of the equation.

Beta particles are not good ionisers because they are very light and cannot easily strip an electron from an atom.

Half-life

Half-life is the time it takes for half the undecayed nuclei in a radioactive substance to decay. If the substance has a very long half-life then it remains active for a very long time.

Atoms in a Sample of Radioactive Substance

○ = Original atom   ● = New atom formed after original atom has decayed

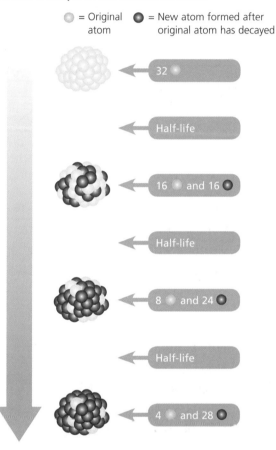

N.B. This is a collection of atoms, not a nucleus.

Calculations Involving Half-life

The half-life of a substance can be calculated using a table or a graph.

Example 1

The table below shows the activity (measured in **becquerels**, **Bq**) of a radioactive substance against time.

Time (min)	0	5	10	15	20	25	30
Activity (Bq)	200	160	124	100	80	62	50

a) Calculate the half-life of the substance by using a table.

To find an average, choose three pairs of points between which the activity has halved.

Activity	Time	Half-Life
200 → 100	0 → 15	15 min
160 → 80	5 → 20	15 min
100 → 50	15 → 30	15 min

The half-life is **15 minutes**.

b) Calculate the half-life by drawing a graph.

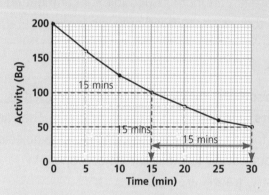

The half-life is **15 minutes**.

Example 2

The half-life of uranium is 4 500 000 000 years. Uranium forms lead when it decays.

A rock sample is found to contain three times as much lead as uranium. Calculate the age of the sample.

The fraction of lead present is $\frac{3}{4}$ while the fraction of uranium present is $\frac{1}{4}$. (There is three times as much lead as uranium.)

Fraction of lead + Fraction of uranium = Original amount of uranium

$$\frac{3}{4} + \frac{1}{4} = 1$$

Work out the number of decays it takes to get $\frac{1}{4}$:

$$1 \xrightarrow{\text{half-life}} \frac{1}{2} \xrightarrow{\text{half-life}} \frac{1}{4} \quad \text{2 half-lives}$$

Age of rock = 2 × half-life

= 2 × 4 500 000 000 years

= **9 000 000 000 years**

Background Radiation

Background radiation occurs **naturally** in our environment and is around us all the time. Most is released by radioactive substances in **soil** and **rocks**. The level of background radiation can vary depending on the rocks in the area. **Cosmic rays** from outer space also contribute significantly to background radiation.

> **HT** Not all background radiation occurs naturally. A small proportion comes from waste products and man-made sources. Industry and hospitals are both responsible for contributing to today's background radiation levels.

Tracers

Radioisotopes (radioactive materials) are used as **tracers** in industry as well as in hospitals. They are used to find out what is happening inside objects without having to break the objects open. In industry, tracers are used to:

- track the dispersal of waste
- find leaks and blockages in underground pipes
- find the routes of underground pipes.

A radioactive material that emits gamma rays is put into the pipe. A gamma source is used because gamma can penetrate through to the surface. The progress of the material is tracked by a detector above ground:

- If there is a leak, the radioactive material will escape and will be detected at the surface.
- If there is a blockage, the radioactive material will stop flowing so it cannot be detected after this point.

Smoke Alarms

Most smoke alarms contain americium-241, which emits alpha particles. The alpha particles cause air particles to ionise and the ions formed are attracted to oppositely charged electrodes in the alarm. This results in a current flowing in the circuit and this means the alarm is working normally.

When smoke enters the space between the two electrodes, the alpha particles are absorbed by the smoke particles and so cannot ionise the air. This causes a smaller current than normal to flow, and the alarm sounds.

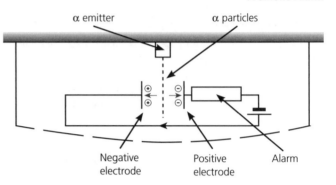

A Smoke Alarm

α emitter   α particles

Negative electrode   Positive electrode   Alarm

Carbon Dating

A small amount of the carbon in our atmosphere and in the bodies of animals and plants is radioactive carbon-14. Measurements from radioactive carbon can be used to date old materials that were once alive.

> **HT** The amount of radioactive carbon-14 in the atmosphere has not changed for thousands of years. When an object dies it no longer exchanges gases with the air like living matter does. Therefore, as the carbon-14 in the dead object decays, the radioactivity of the sample decreases. This means that the dead object has a different radioactivity level to living matter. The ratio of these two activities can be used to find a fairly accurate age within known limits.

Dating Rocks

Rocks were never living things so we cannot find the age of rocks using carbon dating. Instead we look at the amount of naturally occurring radioactive uranium and lead in rocks.

We look at the ratio of uranium to lead in a rock to find out its age. Radioactive uranium has a half life of 4 500 000 000 years. The ratio tells us how long the rock has existed.

Radiation

Although some materials are radioactive naturally, it is possible to make a material radioactive by putting it into a nuclear reactor and allowing it to absorb extra neutrons. This makes its nucleus **unstable** so it emits radiation.

X-rays and **gamma rays** are both electromagnetic waves with similar wavelengths, but they are produced in different ways. X-rays and some nuclear radiation (i.e. **gamma** and **beta radiation**) can be used in medicine. X-rays pass easily through soft tissue and less easily through bone, which produces a shadow image of the insides of the body. The person who takes X-rays and uses radiation is called a **radiographer**.

A radiographer has to take special precautions (e.g. standing behind a lead screen) when X-raying a patient so that he/she does not receive a dangerous accumulated dose of radiation.

Gamma rays damage cells, so they can be used to treat cancer by killing cancerous cells. Beta and gamma rays pass through skin, so they can be used as medical tracers (tracking the tracer's progress through a patient's system) to help diagnose problems such as blood clots. Gamma rays can also be used to **sterilise** medical equipment because they kill germs and bacteria.

It is important that radioactive tracers do not remain in the body for long so that patients do not irradiate other people. This means that tracers must have a suitable half-life.

HT X-rays are made by firing high-speed electrons at metal targets. (The electrons lose energy very quickly.) X-rays are easier to control than gamma rays.

Gamma rays are frequently given out after alpha or beta decay. The nucleus sometimes contains surplus energy after emitting alpha or beta particles. It emits this extra energy as gamma radiation, which is very high frequency electromagnetic radiation. Unlike alpha or beta decay, gamma has no effect on the structure of the nucleus.

HT Uses of Gamma Rays

Treating Cancer

A wide beam of gamma rays is focused on the tumour. The beam is rotated around the outside of the body with the tumour at the centre of rotation. This concentrates the gamma rays on the tumour, but minimises damage to the rest of the body. Gamma radiation treatment destroys cancer cells without surgery. But, it may damage other (healthy) cells and cause sickness.

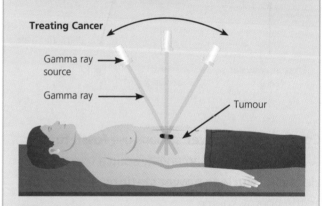

Treating Cancer

Gamma ray source

Gamma ray

Tumour

Tracers

A tracer is a small amount of a radioactive material which is put into a patient so that its progress through the body can be followed using a radiation detector outside the body. The radioactive material must emit either gamma or beta radiation – both of these are capable of passing out of the body to be detected. It must have a short half-life so that the patient does not remain radioactive for long.

The tracer can be swallowed or injected and it is then given time to spread through the patient's body. For example, the thyroid gland is an important organ. Iodine is absorbed in the thyroid gland, so a patient is given a radioactive substance that contains iodine-131. A radiation detector can then be used to follow its progress and find out how well the thyroid gland is working by measuring the amount of iodine it absorbs.

P4 | Fission and Fusion

Fission

Nuclear Power Station

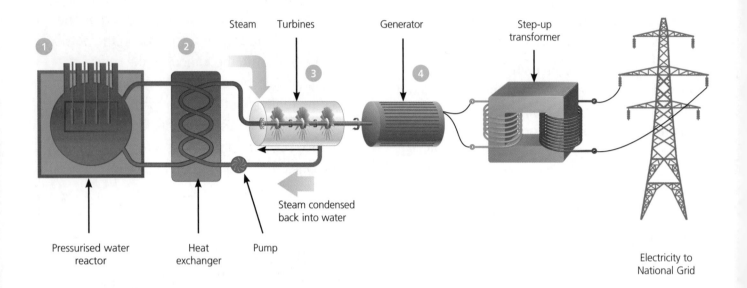

- Steam
- Turbines
- Generator
- Step-up transformer

Steam condensed back into water

Pressurised water reactor

Heat exchanger

Pump

Electricity to National Grid

Conventional power stations use **fossil fuels**, i.e. coal, oil and gas, as an energy source to generate electricity. **Nuclear power stations** use **uranium** as the energy source.

1. A nuclear reaction takes place to produce heat.
2. The heat creates steam from water.
3. The steam turns a turbine.
4. The turbine turns a generator, to produce electricity.

The Nuclear Reaction – Fission

Uranium is used to produce heat energy in a nuclear reactor. The reaction is called **nuclear fission** and this happens in a **chain reaction.** The chain reaction is carefully controlled in a power station.

Absorbing a single neutron is enough to cause a uranium nucleus to split, releasing heat energy and more neutrons. These neutrons cause more uranium nuclei to split and so the chain reaction continues.

Nuclear fission produces radioactive waste. A **nuclear bomb** is a chain reaction that has gone **out of control**, resulting in the release of one powerful burst of energy.

HT Nuclear Fission

Nuclear fission is the process used in nuclear reactors to produce energy to make electricity.

On a Small Scale
Bombarding a uranium atom with a neutron causes the nucleus to split and energy is released as a result.

On a Large Scale
When a neutron collides with a very large nucleus (e.g. uranium), the nucleus splits up into two smaller nuclei (e.g. barium and krypton). This releases more than one neutron, which is capable of causing further fission. This is a chain reaction, so it carries on and on and on.

Scientists stop nuclear reactions getting out of control by putting control rods in the reactor. The control rods absorb some of the neutrons (preventing further fissions). The control rods can be lowered or raised to control the number of neutrons available for fission, which allows the process to keep operating safely.

Small-scale Fission

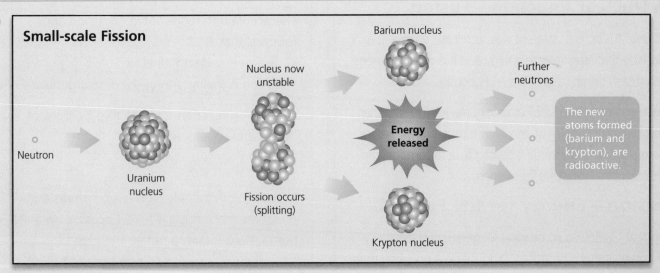

Neutron → Uranium nucleus → Nucleus now unstable / Fission occurs (splitting) → Barium nucleus + Krypton nucleus, Energy released, Further neutrons

The new atoms formed (barium and krypton), are radioactive.

Large-scale Fission

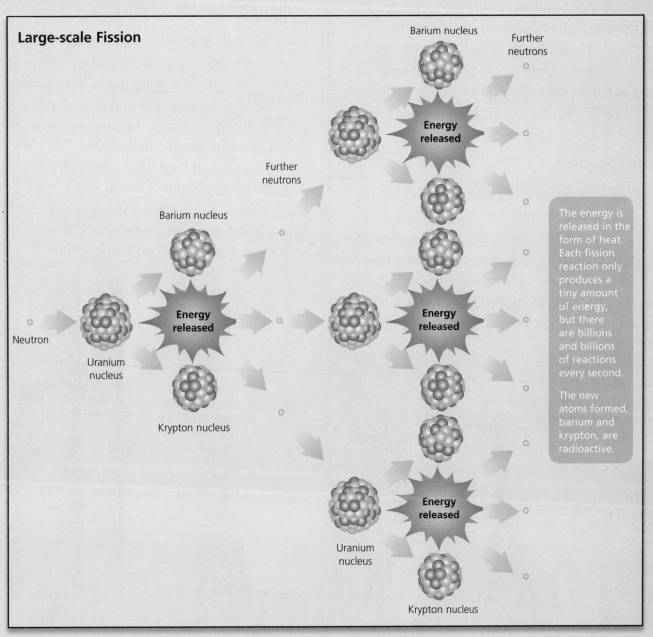

Neutron → Uranium nucleus → Barium nucleus, Energy released, Krypton nucleus, Further neutrons → Barium nucleus, Energy released, Further neutrons, Energy released, Energy released, Uranium nucleus, Energy released, Krypton nucleus

The energy is released in the form of heat. Each fission reaction only produces a tiny amount of energy, but there are billions and billions of reactions every second.

The new atoms formed, barium and krypton, are radioactive.

P4 | Fission and Fusion

A Nuclear Reaction – Fusion

Nuclear fusion is a different way to release energy. It is the way that stars release energy and it is what happens in a fusion bomb (also called an H bomb).

Fusion means two small atomic nuclei joining together. This can only happen at very high temperatures. So, for example, two hydrogen nuclei can fuse to form helium. This reaction releases a lot of energy.

Fusion – Energy for the Future?

Nuclear fusion would be ideal for generating electricity in power stations because it produces less pollution than a fission reactor. However, it is very difficult because it requires extremely high temperatures to get it to work and the components of the power station can melt if they get this hot causing safety problems. Scientists are working to solve this problem at the moment. As it is such a big problem many countries are working together to share costs and expertise.

Cold Fusion?

Two scientists thought they had managed to get fusion to work at room temperature. Many other scientists have tested their claims by trying to get the same experiment to work in their labs (this is how all science is tested). So far no one else has managed to get this to work so the original claims are still not proven and the idea of cold fusion is not accepted.

HT The simple difference between fission and fusion is that:

- fission is splitting an atom
- fusion is joining atoms to form larger ones.

One fusion reaction is to use two isotopes of hydrogen ($^1_1$H) and deuterium ($^2_1$H)

$$^1_1H + {}^2_1H = {}^3_2He$$

In stars the extremely high temperatures and pressures make nuclear fusion possible. In an H bomb it is difficult to obtain the high temperatures so a fission bomb is used to start the fusion reaction.

For generating power, the need to use extremely high temperatures and pressures makes this an inefficient process. This means that, at the moment, if energy is generated using nuclear fusion in a reactor then more energy would be used to create the temperatures and pressures required than would be obtained from the reaction. Scientists are working to overcome the safety and practical challenges so that we may, one day, use fusion to generate clean energy.

1 This is a diagram of a plug.

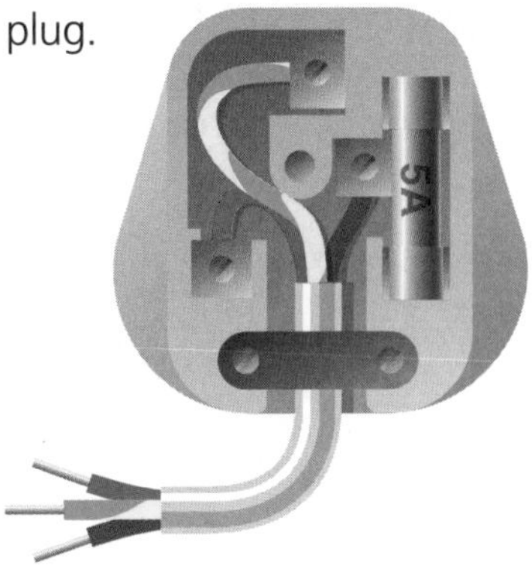

a) Draw lines to match the colour with the type of wire. [3]

Brown		Earth
Green/yellow		Live
Blue		Neutral

b) In a plug you also find a fuse. How does a fuse work? [2]

c) Do double insulated appliances need earthing? Explain your answer. [2]

2 Polonium-210 is a radioactive material. The radioactivity of an object is measured by the number of nuclear decays emitted per second.

a) How does the radioactivity change over time? Tick (✓) the correct answer. [1]

It increases ☐

It decreases ☐

It stays the same ☐

b) Polonium-210 decays by emitting alpha particles from the nucleus. What is an alpha particle? [1]

c) Describe one use of an alpha emitter, and how it works. [2]

HT 3 James rubs a duster over a balloon and both the balloon and the duster become statically charged. The balloon becomes negatively charged.

a) Explain how this happens in terms of electrons. [2]

b) James is then able to stick the balloon to the wall. Explain why he is able to do this. [2]

c) James sometimes finds that when getting out of the car he receives an electric shock. He thinks this is due to static electricity caused by his clothing rubbing against the seat of the car. How can he reduce his chance of getting an electric shock? [2]

Satellites, Gravity and Circular Motion

This module looks at:

- Satellites and their use in global communication.
- How objects move – vectors and equations of motion.
- Projectile motion and the trajectories of objects.
- Momentum and why stopping slowly is safer than a sudden stop.
- The use of microwaves and satellites in transmitting information.
- Wave properties and the interaction of waves, including interference.
- The passage of light as it enters and leaves different materials.
- Cameras and lenses and how they create inverted, real images.

Gravity and Satellites

A **satellite** is an object that orbits a larger object in space. Some satellites are **natural** – for example, the Moon is a natural satellite that orbits the Earth.

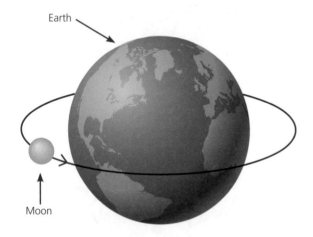

Other satellites are **artificial**, i.e. they have been put in space by humans. A satellite is kept in orbit by a **gravitational force**.

Gravity is a universal force of attraction between masses. Gravity keeps the planets (including the Earth) orbiting the Sun, and keeps the Moon and artificial satellites orbiting the Earth.

Centripetal Force

Centripetal force is the force that acts towards the centre of a circle that keeps an object moving in a circle. Gravity provides the centripetal force that keeps a satellite in orbit.

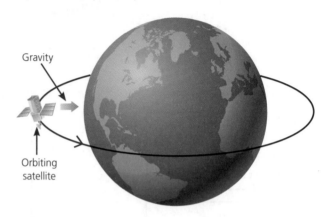

The gravitational force between two objects gets weaker as you move the objects further apart. For example, Mercury is very close to the Sun, so the gravitational force on it is very strong. Mercury travels very fast and orbits quickly. Planets further away from the Sun experience a lower gravitational force and have a longer orbital period.

The gravitational force reduces to a quarter of its strength if the distance between the objects is doubled.

Why do Satellites have Different Orbits?

Low polar orbit satellites are used to look at the Earth's surface. This means they have to be low enough and orbit over the poles while the Earth spins beneath them, so that they can see the Earth segment by segment on each pass to cover the whole Earth. Each orbit takes about 100 minutes.

Communications satellites orbit at the same rate as the Earth, which is once every 24 hours.

Artificial Satellites

Artificial satellites can orbit at different heights above the Earth's surface. The **orbital period** (the time it takes to make one complete orbit) is longer if the satellite is at a higher position above the Earth.

Low Polar Orbit Satellites

The height at which a satellite orbits determines what it can be used for. Satellites in **low polar orbit** travel very quickly and go round the Earth several times each day. They are used for:

- imaging the Earth's surface
- weather forecasting
- military uses (spying).

Geostationary Satellites

Geostationary satellites orbit much higher above the Earth and they take 24 hours to complete one orbit. This means that they remain above a fixed position (above the Equator) on the Earth all the time. They are used for communications, including satellite phone calls, satellite television and weather forecasting. Satellites can also be used for scientific research and global positioning systems (GPS).

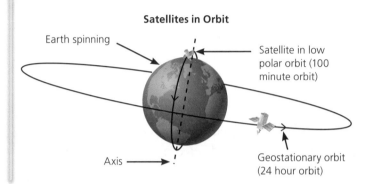

Satellites in Orbit

Earth spinning

Satellite in low polar orbit (100 minute orbit)

Axis

Geostationary orbit (24 hour orbit)

Artificial satellites feel a gravitational force (the centripetal force) accelerating them towards the centre of the Earth. This gravitational force decreases as the distance from Earth increases – the decrease gets greater and greater the further away a satellite is. This is called the inverse square law.

Satellites in low polar orbit feel a strong force, but their speed is fast enough to keep them moving in a circle. It is as if they are trying to fly off at a tangent but are dragged down by gravity, and the two effects balance to cause the satellite to remain in its orbit. This is why it will take a low polar orbit satellite only a few hours to complete one orbit.

Geostationary satellites are in much higher orbits (36000km), therefore the gravitational force on them is weaker. They move more slowly and have further to travel, which is why they take 24 hours to orbit.

Comets

A comet orbits the Sun in an elliptical loop, whereas the planets have almost circular orbits. When a comet is close to the Sun it has to travel very fast to escape the gravitational force, but when it is far away, it travels much more slowly because the Sun's gravity pulls it back.

The effect is the same as when a ball is thrown up into the air: it slows down as it gets higher and speeds up as it gets closer to the Earth – except that comets usually do not crash into the Sun's surface but swing past it.

Orbits of Some of the Planets

Mars   Earth   Venus   Mercury   Sun

Orbit of a Comet

Sun

Comet (tail away from Sun)

Scalar and Vector Quantities

Scalar quantities are those that have a **size** only – for example mass, energy and speed. Direction does not need to be known for these measures.

However, sometimes we need to know about direction. **Vector** quantities, for example, velocity, force, and acceleration, have **size** and **direction**.

Speed

Speed is how fast an object is moving at a particular time, as indicated on a speedometer. Direction is not important when measuring speed. Speed is a scalar quantity.

Velocity

Velocity is how fast an object is moving in a particular direction. Velocity is a vector quantity.

Relative Speed

If two cars are travelling along a road, their motion can be described in terms of their **relative speed**. For example, two cars travelling towards each other have a higher relative speed than two cars travelling in the same direction.

Example 1 (see diagram below)
Car A and Car B are travelling towards each other on a straight road. Each is travelling at 10m/s. The **relative speed** of Car A and Car B is 20m/s. That is, to a person in Car A it will appear as though Car B is travelling towards them at a speed of 20m/s.

Example 2 (see diagram below)
Car C and Car D are travelling in the same direction on a straight road. Car D is travelling at 8m/s and Car C is travelling at 10m/s. Every second, Car C will get 2m closer to Car D, which means that Car C's relative speed is 2m/s.

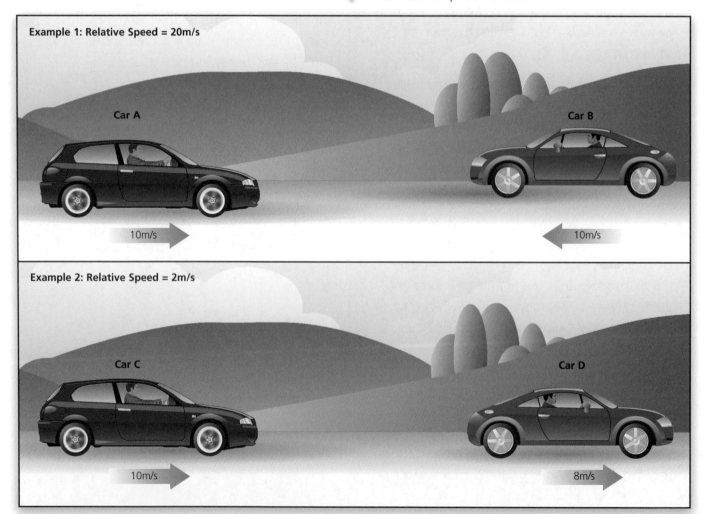

Example 1: Relative Speed = 20m/s

Car A   Car B

10m/s   10m/s

Example 2: Relative Speed = 2m/s

Car C   Car D

10m/s   8m/s

Velocity and Displacement

Velocity and **displacement** (distance travelled in a given direction) can be calculated using these equations:

Final velocity = Initial velocity + (Acceleration × Time)
$v = u + at$

Distance travelled = $\dfrac{\text{(Initial velocity + Final velocity)}}{2}$ × Time
$s = \dfrac{(u + v)}{2} \times t$

u = initial velocity, v = final velocity, a = acceleration, t = time, s = displacement

Example

A bike travelling at 5m/s accelerates at 3m/s^2 for 5 seconds.

a) What is the bike's final velocity?

$v = u + at$
$= 5 + (3 \times 5) = $ **20m/s**

b) How far did the bike travel while accelerating?

$s = \dfrac{(u + v)}{2} \times t$
$= \dfrac{(5 + 20)}{2} \times 5 = $ **62.5m**

Vector Sums

If two forces are acting along the same line (i.e. they are parallel), it is possible to calculate the **total effect** of the two forces from a **vector diagram**:

- Parallel vectors in the same direction add up.

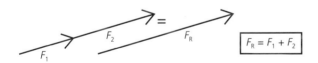

$F_R = F_1 + F_2$

- Parallel vectors in opposite directions subtract.

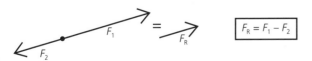

$F_R = F_1 - F_2$

(HT) Resultant Force

If two forces are acting at right angles on the same object, you can work out the **resultant force** by using Pythagoras' Theorem.

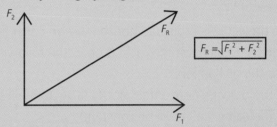

$F_R = \sqrt{F_1^2 + F_2^2}$

N.B. You can work this out using a scale diagram too.

Velocity and Displacement Formulae

The following two formulae can be used to calculate the final velocity of an object, its displacement, its acceleration or the time it was travelling for:

$v^2 = u^2 + 2as$

$s = ut + \dfrac{1}{2}at^2$

Example 1

A runner starts a race and accelerates at 2.5m/s^2 for the first 20m of the race. What is the runner's final velocity?

$v^2 = u^2 + 2as$
$v^2 = 0^2 + 2 \times 2.5 \times 20$
$\quad = 100$
$v = \sqrt{100} = $ **10m/s**

Example 2

A car travelling at 20m/s accelerates at 3m/s^2 for 20 seconds. How far has the car travelled in this time?

$s = ut + \dfrac{1}{2}at^2$
$= (20 \times 20) + (\dfrac{1}{2} \times 3 \times 20^2)$
$= 400 + 600 = $ **1000m**

Projectile Motion

When cannon balls or missiles are fired into the air they are called **projectiles**. Other examples of projectiles are golf balls, footballs, netballs, darts and long-jumpers.

If a projectile is projected horizontally on Earth and there is no air resistance acting on it, the following two things happen:

- the object's horizontal velocity (a vector) will stay the same (i.e. it will be constant).
- the object will accelerate towards the ground so its vertical velocity (a vector) will increase steadily.

This is because, if air resistance is ignored, the only force acting on the projectile is gravity. Gravity can only cause a **downward acceleration** and can only affect the object's vertical velocity. For example, when a stone is kicked horizontally off the edge of a

cliff it will follow a curved **trajectory** (path) as it falls towards the sea. This is because the Earth's gravitational field pulls it towards the ground. This curved trajectory is described as **parabolic**.

How far a ball travels when it is hit or kicked will depend on the angle it was launched at. The ideal angle for maximum distance is 45° above the horizontal.

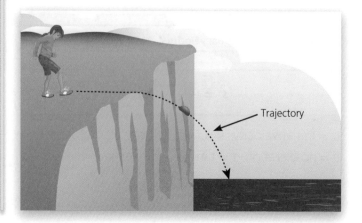
Trajectory

Calculating Projectile Velocity

The horizontal and vertical velocities of a projectile are separate vectors. This means that each motion has its own speed and direction and behaves separately.

The force of gravity is vertical, so it only affects a projectile's vertical velocity but it cannot affect the projectile's horizontal velocity. This is why the horizontal velocity does not change, i.e. there is no acceleration in the horizontal direction.

The projectile's resultant velocity is the vector sum of the horizontal and vertical velocities:

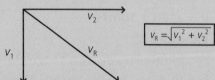

$$v_R = \sqrt{v_1^2 + v_2^2}$$

Example

A stone is kicked off the top of a cliff with a horizontal velocity of 3m/s and lands in the sea 45m below.

a) How long does it take for the stone to hit the surface of the sea?

Vertically, the stone starts with zero velocity and accelerates due to gravity at 10m/s² (see page 45).

$$s = ut + \frac{1}{2}at^2$$
$$45 = (0 \times t) + (\frac{1}{2} \times 10 \times t^2)$$
$$t^2 = \frac{45 \times 2}{10}$$
$$t = \sqrt{9}$$
$$= \textbf{3 seconds}$$

b) What is the velocity of the stone when it hits the sea?

Horizontally the stone's velocity does not change because there is no air resistance. Vertically the stone's velocity increases from its initial velocity of 0m/s, due to gravity.

$$v = u + at$$
$$= 0 + (10 \times t) = 10 \times 3$$
$$= 30\text{m/s vertically}$$

To find the vector sum of the two velocities use Pythagoras' Theorem:

$$v^2 = 3^2 + 30^2 = 909$$
$$v = \sqrt{909} \quad = \textbf{30.1m/s}$$

Actions and Reactions

Wherever there is a **force**, there will be a reaction to the force. It is important to remember that the two forces are equal and act on different objects. Therefore, if gravity is pulling a person down towards the Earth then the person is pulling the Earth towards them with the same force. (However, the Earth does not move as fast as the person does because it is much heavier; $F = ma$)

Collisions

In a **collision**, the velocities of the cars colliding are parallel. This means that if Car A hits Car B with a force, then Car B hits Car A with the same force, even if the two cars are very different sizes. This is why there is damage to both vehicles. The smaller car may recoil more but that is because the same size force has a bigger effect on the smaller mass of the car. For example:

- if a lorry crashes into a car, then the car hits the lorry with the same force
- if a ball is hit with a racquet, then the racquet feels the same force from the ball
- if you hit someone's jaw with your hand, you will also injure your hand because the force on your hand from their jaw is the same as the force from your hand on their jaw.

Rockets – How Do They Get Up There?

When a rocket engine fires, the hot exhaust gases expand rapidly exerting pressure in all directions. The gases are forced out of the back of the rocket and so drive the rocket upwards.

⊞ Conservation of Momentum

If there is a collision or an explosion then the **total momentum** of a system is **conserved**. This means that the total momentum of the system is the same after the event as it was before (though the individual objects in the collision or explosion may have exchanged momentum, i.e. one may have lost momentum and the other may have gained it).

Before a gun is fired, the gun and bullet have a total momentum of zero. After a bullet is fired from the gun, the total momentum is zero because the momentum of the bullet is exactly equal and opposite to the momentum of the gun (recoil). The gun has the same momentum as the bullet, but the bullet moves faster because it has a smaller mass.

This can be worked out using:

$$m_1u_1 + m_2u_2 = m_1v_1 + m_2v_2$$
Where '1' relates to the gun and '2' relates to the bullet.

So if the gun has mass 1 kg and the bullet is 10g and the bullet is fired at 300 m/s from a stationary gun then:

$0 + 0 = (1 \times v_1) + -(0.01 \times 300)$

N.B. The minus sign indicates that the bullet and gun will go in opposite directions. This is because velocity is a vector quantity.

So, the velocity of the gun recoil is v_1 = **3 m/s**.

Explosions

Before an explosion, the total momentum is zero. After an explosion, each fragment flies off in a different direction, so each one has a different momentum. The momentum of one fragment can cancel out the momentum of another fragment (because they are travelling at the same speed in opposite directions), so the total momentum is zero after the explosion, even though every fragment is moving.

Conservation of Momentum (cont)

Rockets

Before a rocket fires its engines, it will have a constant speed. When rocket engines fire briefly in space, the small amount of hot gas that expands is thrown out of the back of the rocket and this has momentum. The momentum of the rocket and gas together is still the same as it was before firing, but the rocket gains momentum (it speeds up) equal to the momentum of the gas backwards.

For this to work when launching a rocket from Earth, the particles of gas must be travelling at high speed and there has to be a very large number of them, but the idea is exactly the same.

Gas Pressure

In a gas, the particles are moving about very quickly all the time so they continually bounce off the sides of the container. This exerts a pressure on the inside of the container – for example, it is the air particles bouncing off the inside of a balloon that keep it inflated.

Adding more gas to a fixed volume container will create a bigger pressure because there are more molecules to hit the walls of the container – for example, pumping more air into a tyre increases its pressure.

Warming up the air in a container will also increase the pressure because each molecule is travelling faster and so it hits the inside of the container harder and more often and this produces a higher pressure.

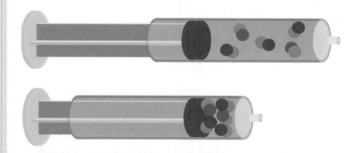

When a gas molecule hits the inside wall of a container, it bounces off and changes its **momentum**. Because force is rate of change of momentum, the gas molecule exerts a force on the container. The faster the molecule is moving (due to the temperature being higher), the greater the change of momentum so the greater the force exerted by each molecule.

If there are more molecules, or they are travelling faster, then the inside walls of the container will experience a greater force because they are being hit more frequently. So, a greater frequency of collisions, due to higher temperature of the gas or increasing the number of molecules in the container, will result in a higher pressure.

Radio Waves

Radio waves are **electromagnetic** waves with low **frequencies** and very long **wavelengths**. They are used to carry information.

Different frequencies of radio waves are affected by the Earth's atmosphere in different ways:

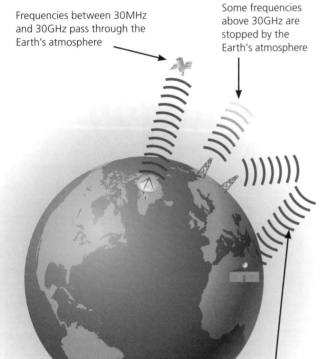

Frequencies between 30MHz and 30GHz pass through the Earth's atmosphere

Some frequencies above 30GHz are stopped by the Earth's atmosphere

Some frequencies are reflected by a part of the Earth's upper atmosphere, the **ionosphere**

Different frequencies of radio waves are used to send information to geostationary satellites than those used to send information to low orbit satellites, because of the difference in their distance from Earth.

Low frequency radio waves are used to communicate with low orbit satellites. Higher frequency waves are used to communicate with higher orbit (geostationary) satellites.

Receiving Programmes

An aerial is needed to pick up a radio or television signal. Satellite signals have much shorter wavelengths. These can only be picked up using a satellite dish. The dish is curved to focus all the microwaves onto the receiver at the centre of the dish.

Radio Waves and the Atmosphere

Radio waves with a frequency below 30MHz (30 megahertz) are reflected by the ionosphere.

Radio waves with frequencies above 30GHz (30 gigahertz) are reduced in strength because they are absorbed and scattered by rain, dust and other effects in the atmosphere.

Radio waves between 30MHz and 30GHz can pass through the Earth's atmosphere.

Microwaves are electromagnetic waves with a higher frequency (shorter wavelength) than radio waves.

Microwaves are used to transmit information to orbiting artificial satellites, which then retransmit information back to Earth.

HT In satellite communication, the microwaves used have a very short wavelength and the size of the dish has to be many times larger than the wavelength of the microwaves in order to capture the waves and focus them onto the receiver. This means they are not likely to be diffracted so the beam remains narrow and focused. This is why the transmitter and receiver have to be well aligned.

In satellite communication, **digital signals** are used. Digital signals are less likely to suffer from interference than analogue signals.

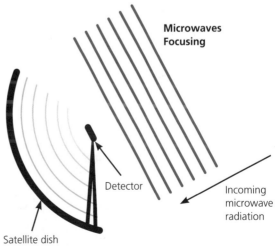

Microwaves Focusing

Detector

Incoming microwave radiation

Satellite dish

Spreading of Radio Waves – Diffraction

If a radio wave passes over a hill or past a large object, it can spread out – this is called **diffraction**. Diffraction makes long wave radio waves more useful for broadcasting television and radio programmes because the waves can get around obstacles.

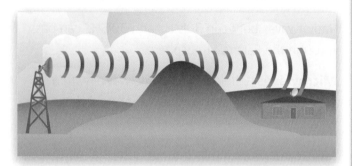

Diffraction can happen to all types of wave if the gap is about the same size as the wavelength of the wave.

For example, a person in a room can hear sounds from outside the room. The wavelength of sound is about the same size as a doorway, so the sound waves spread out as they come through the door. Maximum diffraction happens when the gap is the same size as the wavelength of the wave.

As the gap gets larger, the amount of diffraction gets less, so the wave will tend to go straight through and not diffract through the gap and spread out.

Diffraction helps radio waves to travel around the Earth. Long wavelength radio waves (such as AM BBC Radio 2) have such a long wavelength (over 1km) that they are easily diffracted by hills. This makes it easier to pick up programmes.

Diffraction

1 Gap larger than wavelength – slight diffraction

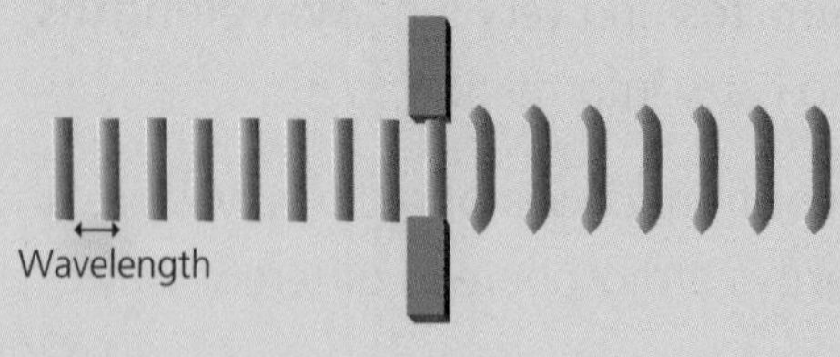

Wavelength

2 Gap about same size as wavelength – maximum diffraction

3 Slight diffraction

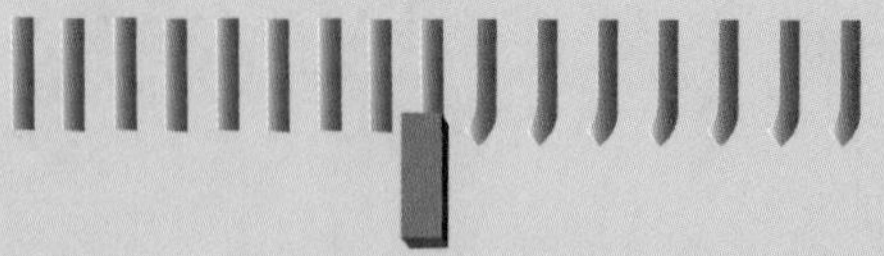

4 Increased diffraction

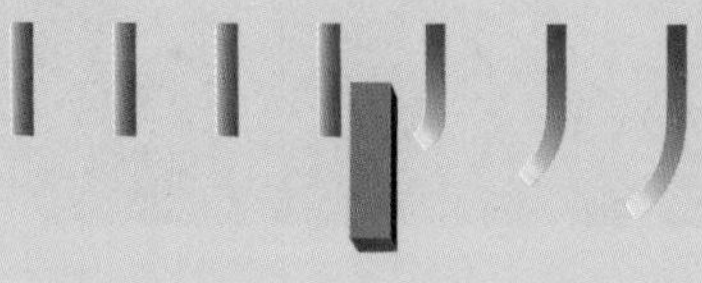

The amount that a wave is diffracted by depends on the size of the gap and the wavelength of the wave:

- Large gaps simply allow the wave to pass straight through without diffracting much. (**1**)
- Maximum diffraction happens when the size of the gap is equal to the wavelength. (**2**)

Microwaves have a short wavelength, which means they do not diffract much round large obstacles. This is why only a thin beam of microwaves is used to transmit information. (**3**)

Radiowaves are long wavelength so bend around large obstacles. (**4**)

Interference

When two **identical** (coherent) waves overlap, the effect produced is called **interference**. Two waves overlapping produce:

- **reinforcement** – areas where waves add together
- **cancellation** – areas where waves subtract from each other.

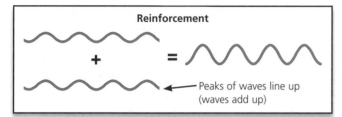

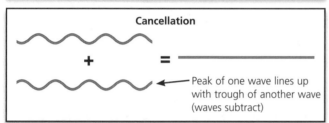

For example, with water waves the area of reinforcement is where the ripples on the surface of the water are deeper. This is because the height of the ripples is made up of two ripples added together. The area of cancellation is where the water surface is flat, because the peak of one wave fills in the trough of the other, cancelling out the waves.

For **sound waves**, interference causes:
- loud areas, where the waves add together
- quiet areas, where the waves subtract from each other.

For **light waves**, interference causes:
- bright areas, where the waves add together
- dark areas, where the waves subtract from each other.

The fact that light can give interference patterns (patches of light and dark) when identical light waves with an identical wavelength overlap, proves that light is a wave. For interference to work the light has to be **coherent**, which means the same wavelength and similar intensity.

N.B. This is not the same interference as on radio programmes, which is 'hissing' or hearing a different programme burst into the one you are listening to.

How Light Travels

Light is an electromagnetic wave and is, therefore, a **transverse** wave that travels in straight lines. The way that an object blocks out light to form a shadow and the Moon blocking out the Sun's light to create an eclipse are evidence of this. However, if light enters a material with a different density at an angle, it changes its speed and this causes it to change direction. This effect is known as **refraction** (see page 10). When light travels through a *very* narrow gap it can spread out into areas it would not otherwise get into (diffraction).

Single Slits and Double Slits

If light from a single wavelength source passes through two closely spaced narrow slits about the same size as the wavelength of light, then two beams will diffract and overlap to create an interference pattern.

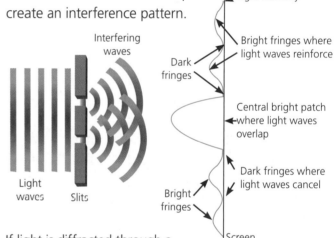

If light is diffracted through a single slit it is still possible to get an interference pattern because beams of light from different parts of the wave front can overlap and create destructive and constructive patterns. Interference of light is evidence that light is a wave because only waves can interfere.

Polarisation

Light waves, like all electromagnetic waves, are **transverse** waves. This means that the oscillation is at 90° to the direction that the wave is travelling. Only transverse waves can be **plane polarised**. This means that if there is a horizontal polariser, then only the horizontal oscillations can get through; the rest are absorbed by the material.

HT Polarisation (cont)

Polarisation is used in some sunglasses to cut out glare from sunlight. They do this by absorbing light that is reflected from shiny surfaces (e.g. the surface of water) where the oscillations of the light wave are in certain directions. This means that the light that gets through the sunglasses is 'plane polarised' (its oscillations are in only one direction) and, therefore, less bright.

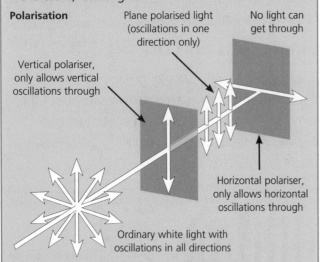

Polarisation

Plane polarised light (oscillations in one direction only)

No light can get through

Vertical polariser, only allows vertical oscillations through

Horizontal polariser, only allows horizontal oscillations through

Ordinary white light with oscillations in all directions

Constructive and Destructive Interference

An interference pattern for light (see page 79) is caused by light from two different but coherent sources overlapping and causing either **constructive** interference or **destructive** interference.

The two waves could come from the same source but two different very small slits (same size as the wavelength of light) which cause the waves to diffract and overlap to reinforce or cancel.

When identical waves (**coherent**) arrive **in phase** at a point, there is constructive interference. This produces a wave with a larger amplitude. When identical waves arrive **out of phase** at a point, there is destructive interference. This causes the amplitude of the resulting wave to be zero.

Coherent waves have to have the same frequency, the same amplitude and be in phase.

Path Difference

Even though two coherent waves come from the same source, they may have taken different paths to reach an object – for example, one wave could have reflected off a mirror while the other took a direct path to the screen.

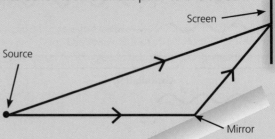

Screen

Source

Mirror

If this happens, then the **path difference** needs to be calculated. The path difference is:

- an **odd** number of half wavelengths for **destructive** interference – the waves cancel
- an **even** number of half wavelengths for **constructive** interference – the waves reinforce.

History of Light

Many years ago people thought that light was made of particles given out by your eyes so that you could see any object the particles bounced off. This could explain reflection as particles bouncing off the surface, but could not explain refraction or diffraction. The wave idea can explain all these things.

HT Science progresses by people criticising existing theories and providing better explanations for the things that they have observed. One good example is the experiment where light was seen to cause interference patterns for the first time. This caused scientists to review their theories about light and agree on a model that describes light as a wave.

Refraction

Light can travel through transparent materials. A transparent material is known as a **medium** (plural is **media**).

When light travels from one medium to another at an angle to the **normal** (i.e. the line at 90° to the surface), for example, from air into glass, it will change direction. This is known as **refraction** (bending).

Refraction occurs at the boundary between two media due to a change in the wave speed. For example, glass is more optically dense than air so the light slows down in glass. If the wave speed slows down, then the light is refracted towards the normal as it enters the material. The angle at which the light ray continues in the second medium is known as the **angle of refraction**. This depends on the angle at which the light hits the boundary between the media, i.e. the **angle of incidence**, and on how much it is refracted (changes speed).

When a ray of light travels from air into glass, the angle of incidence is greater than the angle of refraction because it slows down.

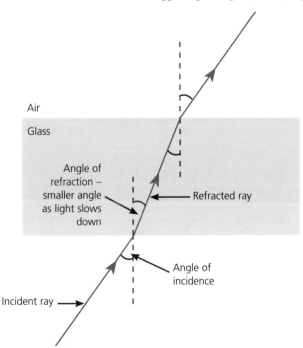

Refracted ray (parallel to incident ray) – bigger angle as light speeds up again

Air

Glass

Angle of refraction – smaller angle as light slows down

Refracted ray

Angle of incidence

Incident ray

Refractive Index

A **refractive index** is a way of measuring how much the light changes speed and, therefore, how much it is refracted as it enters or leaves a new medium.

The amount of refraction increases when there is a greater change in the wave speed and refractive index.

For example, glass has a bigger refractive index than water, so light travelling from air into glass is refracted more (slows down more) than light travelling from air into water.

Refractive index is calculated by:

$$\text{Refractive index} = \frac{\text{Speed of light in vacuum}}{\text{Speed of light in medium}}$$

Example

If light travels at 3×10^8m/s in a vacuum and 2×10^8m/s in glass, what is the refractive index of glass?

$$\text{Refractive index} = \frac{3 \times 10^8}{2 \times 10^8}$$

$$= 1.5 \quad \longleftarrow \quad \text{No units}$$

Dispersion

Light is made up of the colours of the **spectrum** (rainbow).

The spectral colours have different wavelengths, so when light travels through a prism, each colour is slowed down and refracted by different amounts.

Blue light is slowed down the **most** and red light is slowed down the least. This means that blue light changes direction (is refracted) more than red light.

This causes **dispersion** and produces the colours of the spectrum – red, orange, yellow, green, blue, indigo, violet.

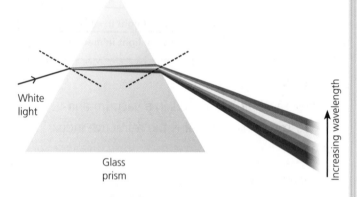

Critical Angle

Different media have different **critical angles**. The critical angle is the maximum angle of incidence (measured from the normal) at which light can exit from a material after refraction.

At angles larger than the critical angle, all the light is reflected back into the material – this is called total internal reflection.

N.B. The critical angle of a medium depends upon its ability to refract, i.e. its refractive index. A big refractive index gives a smaller critical angle.

Internal Reflection

Not all light is refracted when it leaves glass or water to travel through air. Some of the light is reflected from the surface. This is called **internal reflection**.

The amount that light is reflected depends on the angles involved:

- If there is a **small angle of incidence** in a medium, most of the light is refracted and gets out into the air:

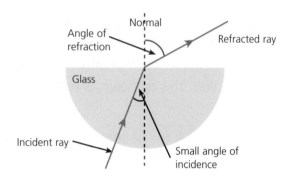

- If there is a **larger angle of incidence** in a medium, more light is reflected and less gets out into the air.
- If light hits the boundary at the **critical angle**, it is refracted, so it emerges at **90° to the normal**:

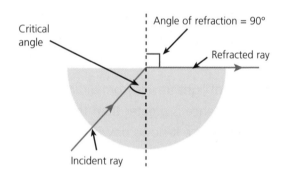

- If the angle of incidence is **larger than the critical angle**, no light is refracted, i.e. all the light is reflected back into the medium. This is known as **total internal reflection**:

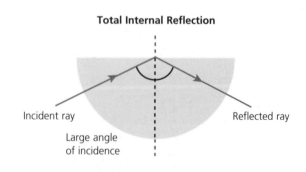

Different media have different critical angles.

Total Internal Reflection

Total internal reflection happens when light is reflected inside a transparent material. It is used in optical fibres, binoculars, bicycle reflectors, cats' eyes in the road and road signs.

Examples of Total Internal Reflection

Optical Fibres

Light travels along a transparent glass or plastic optical fibre by total internal reflection. The light reflects off the sides of the fibre.

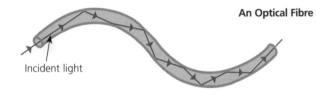

An Optical Fibre

Incident light

Bicycle Reflectors

The light undergoes total internal reflection at the plastic–air boundary and leaves the reflector parallel to the ray of light entering.

A Bicycle Reflector

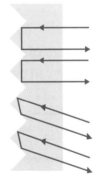

Cats' Eyes

Cats' eyes are reflectors used to show lane markings on roads.

They consist of reflective glass set within a rubber dome, which is protected from traffic inside a metal casing.

Cats' Eyes and Reflection

Light to driver to show
cats' eye in the road

Light from headlights

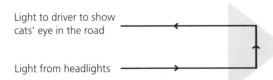

At the critical angle, light in a medium will refract at 90° as it exits. Above the critical angle, the light will not be able to refract (it cannot refract at an angle larger than 90°). At this point, it undergoes total internal reflection inside the medium.

Total internal reflection only occurs when light is going from a medium with a high refractive index to one with a lower refractive index. This is because the effect relies on the light being refracted away from the normal as the light ray speeds up, and the angle of incidence is greater than the critical angle.

The higher the refractive index of light, the smaller the critical angle (the medium is more effective at refracting).

More about Dispersion

Light is dispersed when it enters glass because blue light has a shorter wavelength and it is slowed down more than red light.

So, blue light's wavelength is reduced more and deviated more than other colours of light.

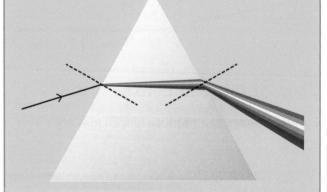

Glass has a higher refractive index for blue light than for red light.

Convex Lenses

A **convex** lens is called a **converging** lens because when light rays pass through it, they converge. When a light ray **parallel** to the axis passes through a convex lens, it will all pass through the **focal point** (focus).

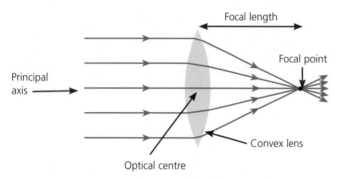

The **focal length** of a convex lens is the distance between the centre of the lens and the focal point.

Fatter lenses refract light more, therefore they have shorter focal lengths. If a diverging beam of light hits a convex lens, the light will converge but not hit the focal point. (However, it is possible that the diverging beam will hit the lens and emerge as a parallel beam if the focal length of the lens is just right.)

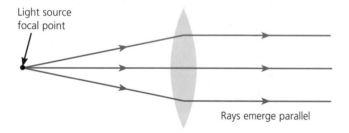

Uses of Convex Lenses

Convex lenses can produce real images on a screen.

Cameras and projectors also use convex lenses. They create a **real image** on a screen:

- in a camera the screen is at the back of a camera (either the film or the CCD detector)
- for a projector the screen is in front of the projector.

Camera

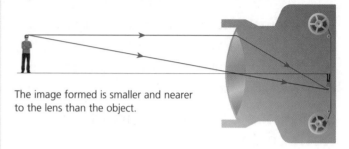

The image formed is smaller and nearer to the lens than the object.

Projector

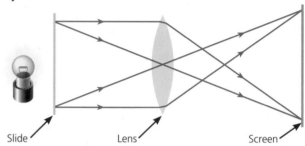

To focus the image in a camera or projector it is important to ensure that rays of light from each point on the object pass through the lens and then meet on the screen. The lens can be moved back and forth to do this (focusing).

Magnification

Magnification is a measure of how much bigger an image is than the object. It can be calculated using the following formula:

$$\text{Magnification} = \frac{\text{Image size}}{\text{Object size}}$$

Convex lenses can be used as magnifying glasses and in spectacles for long-sighted people.

Example
An object 2mm wide appears to be 5mm wide when viewed through a magnifying glass. What is the magnification of the magnifying glass?

$$\text{Magnification} = \frac{\text{Image size}}{\text{Object size}}$$

$$= \frac{5mm}{2mm}$$

$$= 2.5 \quad \longleftarrow \quad \boxed{\text{No units}}$$

Ray Diagrams

Real images can be projected onto a screen and are always inverted.

When light travels through a lens it is **refracted**:

- Light parallel to the principal axis will be refracted to pass through the focal point.
- Light that has passed through the focal point will be refracted to emerge from the lens parallel to the principal axis.
- Light that passes through the centre of the lens is not refracted so passes straight through.

These facts can be used to draw ray diagrams to find the position and size of an image.

1 Draw a ray straight through the centre of the lens.

2 Draw a ray from the top of the object (O) parallel to the axis, as far as the lens.

3 Draw a ray from this point in the lens through the focal point (F).

4 The point at which the rays join is the top of the image (I) on the screen.

N.B. The image will be inverted.

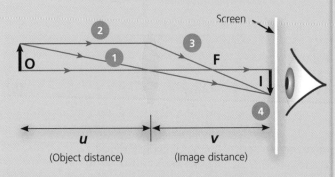

(Object distance) u

(Image distance) v

Light Refracted as if Through a Prism

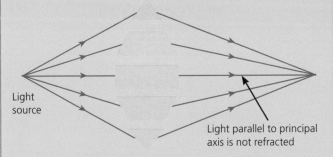

Light source

Light parallel to principal axis is not refracted

Virtual images cannot be projected onto a screen and are the right way up.

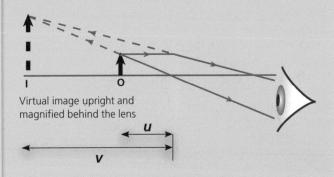

Virtual image upright and magnified behind the lens

u

v

Looking through a magnifying glass you will see a virtual enlarged (magnified) image.

P5 Exam Practice Questions

1. If a girl who has a mass of 70kg stands on the Earth, where the gravitational force is approximately 10N/kg she weighs 700N.

   a) What is her weight if she stands on the Moon where the gravitational force is 2N/kg? **[2]**

   b) Gravity pulls us to the Earth, preventing us from floating around like astronauts do in space stations. Define gravity. **[1]**

   c) Gravity also holds satellites in their orbit. What is a satellite? **[1]**

   d) Give two uses of artificial satellites. **[2]**

2. Look at this diagram.

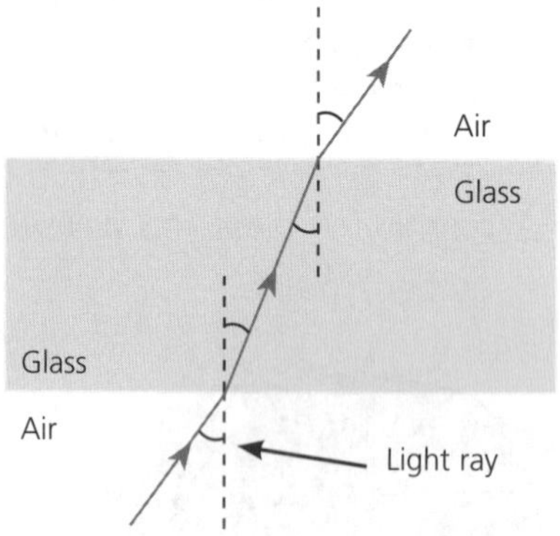

   a) What is happening to the light ray in the diagram? Tick (✓) the correct option. **[1]**

It is being reflected	☐	It is being dispersed	☐
It is being refracted	☐	It is being diffracted	☐

   b) Explain why this happens. **[2]**

   c) The speed of the light in a vacuum is 3×10^8m/s. The speed of light in glass is around 2×10^8m/s. Calculate the refractive index of glass. **[2]**

HT 3. Some quantities are scalar and some are vector.

   a) State whether each of these quantities is a scalar or a vector quantity. **[5]**

   Mass; Force; Velocity; Time; Acceleration.

   b) A car starts from stationary and speeds up to 4m/s in 3 seconds. Calculate the distance the car travels in 3 seconds. **[2]**

   c) Calculate the acceleration of the car. **[2]**

P6: Electricity for Gadgets

This module looks at:

- How controls can be built into the circuits of electrical devices.
- How fixed and variable resistors, LDRs and thermistors are used in circuits to control the potential difference output.
- Logic circuits and gates in electronic devices such as computers.
- How truth tables can be created to show combinations of logic gates.
- Electric motors in electronic devices and how magnetic fields produce movement.
- Electricity as a form of energy, and how it is generated.
- Electricity and different voltages, including how voltage is adjusted by transformers.
- Alternating and direct current and the use of diodes and capacitors.

Circuit Symbols

The following **symbols** are used to represent components in **circuits**:

Resistor		**Battery**	
Variable resistor		**Switch (open)**	
Bulb		**Relay**	
Cell		**Power supply**	(DC) (AC)
Thermistor		**LDR**	
Diode		**LED**	

Resistors

A **resistor** in a circuit resists the flow of current. A **variable resistor** can have its resistance changed. It can be used to:

- control current by increasing or decreasing its resistance – higher resistance gives a lower current
- vary the brightness of a bulb by changing the current – higher current gives a brighter bulb
- vary the speed of a motor by changing the current – higher current gives greater speed.

Ohm's Law

The following units are used for electrical circuits:

- **voltage** is measured in **volts** (V)
- **current** is measured in **amps** (A)
- **resistance** is measured in **ohms** (Ω).

For a given **ohmic** conductor, the current increases as the voltage increases. The **current** in a wire is a flow of **charge carriers** called **electrons**. Resistance in a wire happens when the charge carriers (electrons) collide with the atoms in the conductor and slow down.

Resistance can be calculated using the formula:

$$\text{Resistance } (\Omega) = \frac{\text{Voltage (V)}}{\text{Current (A)}}$$

Examples

If a device carries a current of 0.2A with a voltage of 12V across it, what is its resistance?

$$\text{Resistance} = \frac{\text{Voltage}}{\text{Current}}$$

$$= \frac{12V}{0.2A}$$

$$= 60\Omega$$

Resistance and Temperature

When a wire gets hot, its resistance increases. This means that the hotter a wire gets, the higher its resistance and the lower the current that can flow through it for a given voltage.

Resistance and Temperature (cont)

A longer wire in a rheostat (variable resistor) gives a higher resistance because each charge carrier (electron) is more likely to collide with an atom in the wire and slow down.

More collisions result in higher resistance.

Voltage–Current Graphs for Ohmic Conductors

The **voltage–current graph** below is for an **ohmic conductor**.

The gradient of the graph shows the resistance (in ohms) of the conductor:

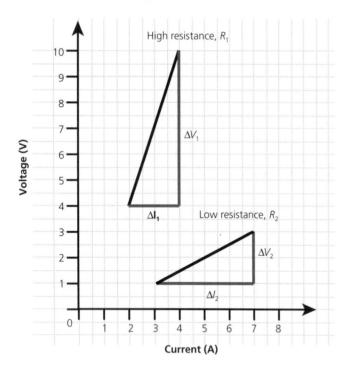

$$R_1 = \frac{\Delta V_1}{\Delta I_1} = \frac{10-4}{4-2} = \frac{6}{2} = 3\Omega$$

$$R_2 = \frac{\Delta V_2}{\Delta I_2} = \frac{3-1}{7-3} = \frac{2}{4} = 0.5\Omega$$

So, R_1 is a higher resistance than R_2.

Voltage–Current Graphs for Non-Ohmic Conductors

The graph below shows the **voltage–current graph for a non-ohmic conductor**, for example, a filament bulb. The increasing gradient shows that the resistance increases as the current increases:

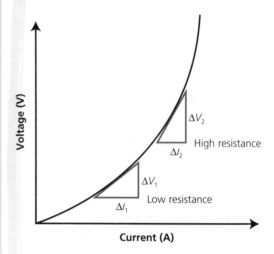

As the temperature of the filament rises, the atoms vibrate more and so there are more collisions with the charge carriers (electrons) and so the charge flow is impeded more and there is a higher resistance.

As the temperature of a resistor rises, its resistance increases because there is an increase in the number of collisions between charge carriers (electrons) and atoms.

These collisions then cause the atoms to vibrate more and this results in an increase in temperature of the conductor. This is the reason why the *V–I* graph for a filament bulb is curved.

The curve shows an increase in gradient as the current rises, showing that the resistance is increasing.

The resistance of the resistor can be calculated from the graph by calculating the gradient of a tangent at a particular point – see the diagrams above.

Potential Dividers

A **potential divider** can be made of **fixed resistors** that are arranged so that they produce the **potential difference (pd)** output needed.

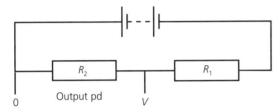

In the example above, there is a pd across each of the two fixed resistors. If a connection is made across one of the two fixed resistors, the pd across that resistor is the output (fed to another device to power it). The output depends on the relative sizes of the two resistors, R_1 and R_2.

Resistors in Series

If there are two (or more) resistors in series in a circuit, then to calculate the total resistance simply add the separate resistances:

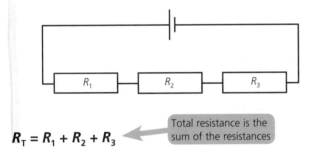

$$R_T = R_1 + R_2 + R_3$$

Total resistance is the sum of the resistances

Potential Dividers with Variable Resistors

If a **variable resistor** is used in a potential divider, the exact pd of the output from the circuit can be chosen. The lower its resistance, the lower the pd output.

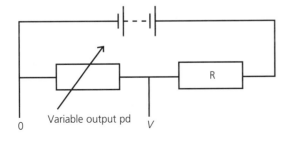

The output pd reduces as the resistance of the variable resistor is reduced, giving a controllable output to power a device.

Resistors in Parallel

If there are two or more resistors in parallel in a circuit, then the total resistance of the circuit is less than the smallest of the separate resistors.

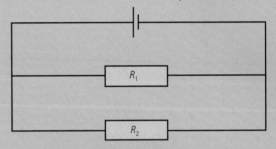

Here, the total resistance is **less** than either R_1 or R_2. Putting resistors in parallel reduces the overall resistance of the circuit.

To calculate the total resistance:

$$\frac{1}{R_T} = \frac{1}{R_1} + \frac{1}{R_2} + \dots$$

Example

In the circuit below, calculate the total resistance.

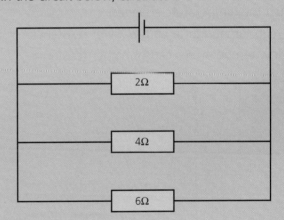

$$\frac{1}{R_T} = \frac{1}{R_1} + \frac{1}{R_2} + \frac{1}{R_3}$$

$$\frac{1}{R_T} = \frac{1}{2} + \frac{1}{4} + \frac{1}{6}$$

$$= \frac{6 + 3 + 2}{12} = \frac{11}{12}$$

$$R_T = \frac{12}{11} \text{ ohms}$$

Light Dependent Resistors

(3) A **light dependent resistor** (LDR) changes its resistance in different light levels:

- bright light causes lower resistance.
- dim light causes higher resistance.

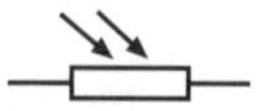

Symbol for LDR

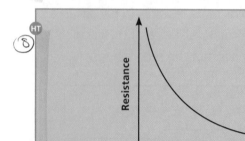

Using an LDR in place of a fixed resistor in a potential divider gives an output signal that depends on light conditions.

For example, bright light causes a low voltage because the resistance of the LDR is lower than that of the fixed resistor in the potential divider.

Thermistors

Symbol for thermistor

(4) A **thermistor** changes its resistance when the temperature changes:

- high temperatures causes lower resistance
- low temperatures causes higher resistance.

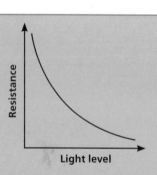

Using a thermistor as the variable resistor in a potential divider gives an output signal that depends on the temperature.

For example, a higher temperature causes a lower voltage because the resistance of the thermistor is lower than that of the fixed resistor in the potential divider.

Calculating Output PDs

(6) The **output** pd from a potential divider can be calculated using the formula:

$$\text{Output pd } V_{out} = \frac{R_2}{(R_1 + R_2)} \times V_{in}$$

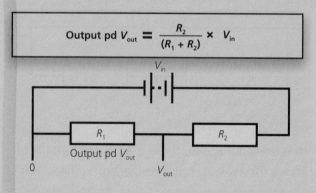

Example

A 20Ω resistor and a 30Ω resistor are connected in series with a 100V supply to make a potential divider. What is the output across the 20Ω resistor?

$$V_o = \frac{20}{20 + 30} \times 100$$

$$= 0.4 \times 100$$

$$= \mathbf{40V}$$

Variable Outputs

(7) A variable resistor can be used instead of a fixed resistor. This will give an output pd that can be **adjusted** to provide the voltage required to operate the chosen device.

The voltage can range from zero to almost the total voltage of the circuit (depending on how big the variable resistor can be).

When R_1 is very much greater than R_2 then the value of V_{out} is approximately V_{in}.

When R_1 is very much less than R_2 then the value of V_{out} is approximately zero. A variable resistor in place of R_1 can provide an output that is completely adjustable between zero and V_{in}.

Transistors

The **transistor** is the basic building block of electronic components. An average computer will have millions (if not billions) of transistors inside on the 'chips'.

A transistor is an electronic switch.

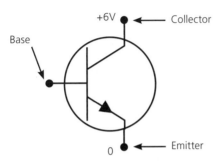

A current can flow through the transistor from the collector to the emitter (in the direction of the arrow) if there is a small current fed to the base. The base current can be very small but it can switch on and off a large current through the collector and emitter.

The current from the emitter is calculated as:

$$I_e = I_b + I_c$$

I_e is emitter current
I_b is base current
I_c is collector current

> **HT** In the circuit below, when there is a current on the base, then current flows through the transistor and will switch on the LED.
>
> There is a large resistance in the base circuit to ensure that the current onto the base is kept small.
>
>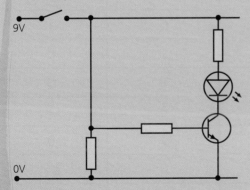
>
> It is important to remember this circuit diagram and be able to draw it and label it.

Transistors and Logic Gates

Transistors can be connected together to make **logic gates**. Logic gates are designed to give a particular output signal (on or off – high or low) when a particular input signal (or combination of two input signals), high or low is fed to it.

Inputs and Logic Gates

The input to a logic gate can be:
- a high voltage (about 5V) – called **high** – or 1
- a low voltage (about 0V) – called **low** – or 0.

The output (Q) of a logic gate is either high or low, depending on its input signal(s).

The circuit below shows two transistors connected so that they act as an **AND gate**:

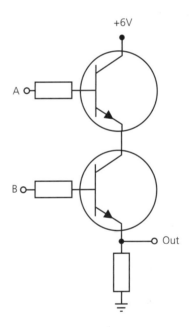

It is important to remember this circuit and recognise it as an AND gate.

The AND gate gives a high output when A and B are both high. This allows current to flow because both transistors are switched ON.

Other logic gates can be made from different combinations of transistors.

Logic Gates and Truth Tables

The output from a logic gate is set out as a 'truth table'. The truth tables for some logic gates are shown below.

Gate	Truth Table		

NOT gate – gives out the **opposite** of the input.

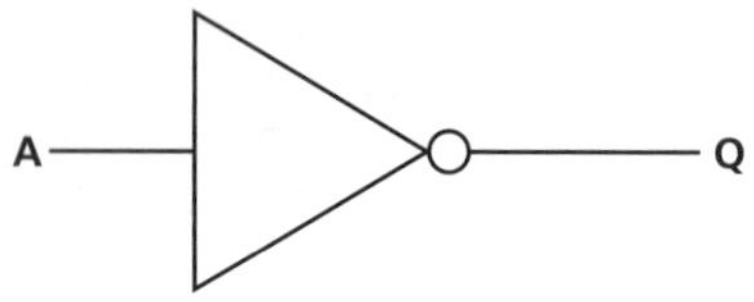

A (Input)		Q (Output)	
0		1	
1		0	

AND gate – gives a high output if the input on input A **and** input B are high.

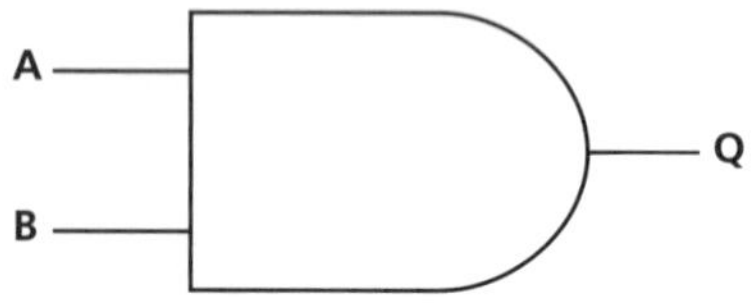

A	B	Q
0	0	0
0	1	0
1	0	0
1	1	1

OR gate – gives a high output if input A **or** input B is high.

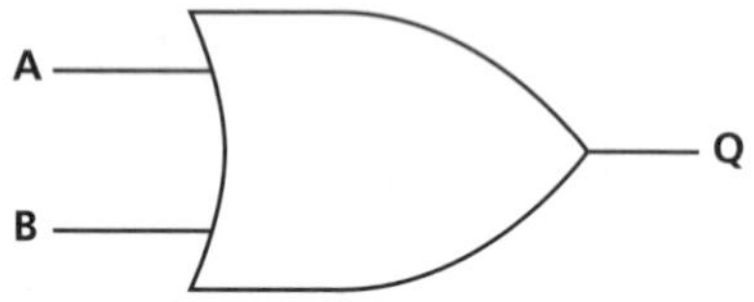

A	B	Q
0	0	0
0	1	1
1	0	1
1	1	1

NAND gate – an AND gate and a NOT gate in series. The output is the **opposite of an AND** gate.

A	B	Q
0	0	1
0	1	1
1	0	1
1	1	0

NOR gate – an OR gate and a NOT gate in series. The output is the **opposite of an OR** gate.

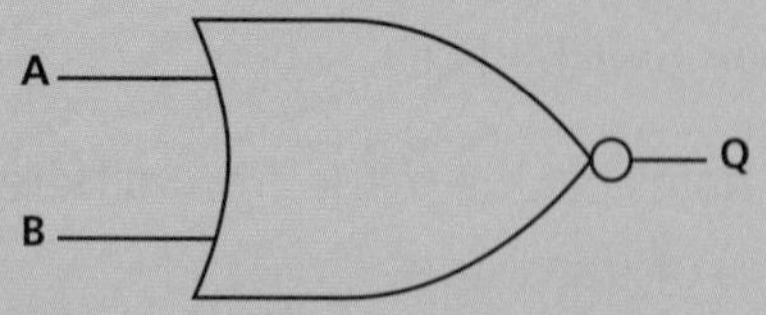

A	B	Q
0	0	1
0	1	0
1	0	0
1	1	0

Complex Truth Tables

A **truth table** can be made for a logic system with three (or more) inputs, in order to work out what the final output is for any combination of inputs.

For example, the diagram below shows an AND gate connected to an OR gate. The truth table for this combination is shown below.

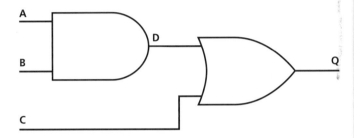

To complete a truth table, fill in all the possible inputs (A, B, C), then work out each output in turn – D then Q.

A	B	C	D	Q
0	0	0	0	0
0	0	1	0	1
0	1	0	0	0
0	1	1	0	1
1	0	0	0	0
1	0	1	0	1
1	1	0	1	1
1	1	1	1	1

Hint: Fill in the inputs (A, B and C) in the table by counting up in binary code – i.e. 000, 001, 010, 011, 100, 101, 110, 111. This way you don't miss any. Then take the logic gates in turn to work out the output D for each, and finally the overall output Q for each.

LEDs as Outputs

The output from a logic gate can switch on a **light emitting diode** (**LED**). This means that when the logic gate gives a positive (high) output, the LED lights up. For example, this could be used to show that a heater has come on.

An LED emits light when a voltage is fed to it. This means it can be used to indicate the output of a logic gate. An LED requires only a very small current, so a resistor is put in series with the LED to ensure that the current through it is small enough.

A **relay** can be used as a switch. A small current in the relay coil switches on a circuit in which a larger current flows.

> (HT) A relay is needed for a logic gate to switch on a larger current in a mains circuit because it works at the same low voltage as logic gates and keeps the low voltage circuit separate from the high voltage mains circuit.

> (HT) **More about Truth Tables**
>
> In your exam you may be asked to work through a logic system made of logic gates to work out a truth table.
>
> You should set up the inputs, (A, B, C, D, etc.) and then fill in the truth table using binary code (i.e. 0 and 1).
>
> The output for a logic gate should be worked out for each pair of inputs. Then the process should be repeated for each logic gate until the final outputs have been found.

More about Truth Tables (cont)

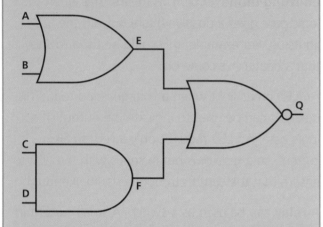

A	B	C	D	E	F	Q
0	0	0	0	0	0	1
0	0	0	1	0	0	1
0	0	1	0	0	0	1
0	0	1	1	0	1	0
0	1	0	0	1	0	0
0	1	0	1	1	0	0
0	1	1	1	1	1	0
1	0	0	0	1	0	0
1	0	0	1	1	0	0
1	0	1	0	1	0	0
1	0	1	1	1	1	0
1	1	0	0	1	0	0
1	1	0	1	1	0	0
1	1	1	1	1	1	0

Hint: Note that the same strategy has been used to fill in this truth table.

First the possible binary codes for inputs A, B, C and D. Then the outputs E and F; and finally the set of possible overall outputs Q.

Inputs for Logic Gates

To get the high or low input for a logic gate we can use switches, LDRs and thermistors as input sensors. For example, an LDR will provide a 'high' input when the LDR has a low resistance, i.e. when it is in the light.

A thermistor will give a 'high' input when the thermistor has a low resistance, i.e. when it is hot.

In both cases a fixed resistor is put in series so that the actual voltage on the logic gate input is kept to only 5V.

Thermistor

Light dependent resistor

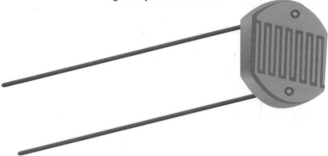

Putting an LDR or thermistor in series with a variable resistor in a potential divider can make an input for the logic gate that switches to high at exactly the right light level or temperature. It makes the circuit completely adjustable.

Magnetic Field Around a Straight Wire

A wire carrying an electric current has a circular **magnetic field** around it, which is made up of concentric circles (cylinders along its length).

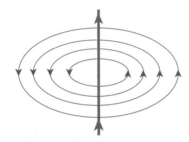

If the wire is put near to a magnet, the two magnetic fields interact and the wire can move.

Magnetic Field Around a Rectangular Coil

The magnetic field around a rectangular coil forms straight lines through the centre of the coil.

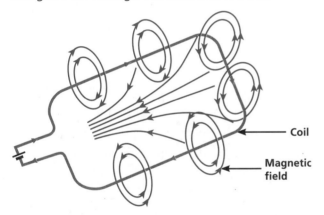

Coil

Magnetic field

Magnetic Field Around a Solenoid

The magnetic field around a **solenoid** looks like the magnetic field around a bar magnet.

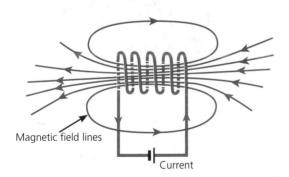

Magnetic field lines

Current

Wires Moving in Magnetic Fields

For a wire in a magnetic field to experience a maximum **force**, it has to be at **right angles** to the magnetic field. The exact direction it moves in depends on the direction of the current and the direction of the magnetic field. The direction that the wire moves in can be reversed by:

- reversing the direction of the magnetic field
- reversing the direction of the current in the wire.

HT Fleming's Left-hand Rule

Fleming's left-hand rule can be used to predict the direction of the force on a current-carrying wire. The rule states that if your first finger points in the direction of the magnetic field and your second finger points in the direction of the current, then your thumb will point in the direction of the force on the wire, making it move.

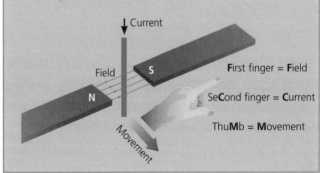

Current

Field

S

N

Movement

First finger = **F**ield

Se**C**ond finger = **C**urrent

Thu**M**b = **M**ovement

Coils Rotating in Magnetic Fields

When a rectangular coil is placed in a magnetic field, it will rotate when it carries a current.

- The current flowing through the coil will create a magnetic field.
- The magnetic field of the magnet and the magnetic field of the coil will interact.
- Each side of the coil will experience a force in opposite directions because the current is flowing in opposite directions in the two parts of the coil.
- The forces will combine to make the coil rotate.

Coils Rotating in Magnetic Fields (cont)

A simple **direct current** (DC) electric **motor** works by having a rectangular coil placed in a magnetic field, causing it to rotate.

The speed of a motor can be altered by changing:
- the size of the electric current (higher current makes it turn faster)
- the number of turns on the coil (more coils makes it turn faster)
- the strength of the magnetic field (a stronger magnet makes it turn faster).

Electric motors are found in many devices, for example:
- washing machines
- CD players
- food processors
- electric drills
- electric lawnmowers
- windscreen wipers
- hairdryers.

Electric motors do useful work because they transfer energy to the load (object being worked on). However, they also transfer energy to the surroundings as wasted energy (heat and sound).

Keeping a DC Motor Going

The direction of the current affects the direction of the force and, therefore, the direction that the motor coil rotates.

The current must always flow in the same direction relative to the magnet in order to keep the coil rotating. A **split-ring commutator** does this by changing the direction of the current in the coil every half turn.

DC Motor

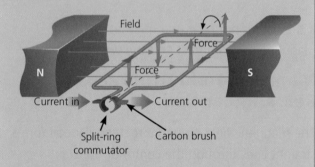

Radial Fields

Because the maximum force is produced when the coil and the field are at right angles to each other, curved pole pieces are used to give a **radial field**. This way, the field lines and the coil are always at the correct angle to give maximum force.

Radial Fields

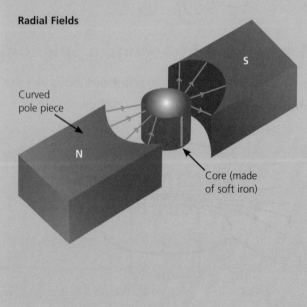

Generating Electricity

Generating electricity is known as the **dynamo effect**. Electricity can be generated by:

- moving a wire near a magnet
- moving a magnet near a wire.

In the UK, electricity is generated at 50 hertz (50Hz). This means the current goes back and forth along the wire 50 times each second (AC).

Inducing Voltages

A voltage is induced across a wire when the wire moves relative to a magnetic field.

A voltage is induced across a coil when the magnetic field within it changes.

If the direction of the changing magnetic field is reversed, the direction of the induced voltage also changes.

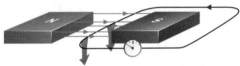

Wire moves down – voltage induced

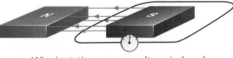

Wire is stationary – no voltage induced

Wire moves up – voltage induced in opposite direction

Alternating Current

An **alternating current** (**AC**) can be generated by rotating a magnet inside a coil of wire. In a power station, the electricity is generated by rotating giant electromagnets inside coils of wire.

Increasing Induced Voltage

The voltage induced can be increased in several ways:

- The speed that the magnet or coil rotates can be increased (this also increases the frequency of the AC).
- The number of turns on the electromagnet's coils (i.e. the number of coils of wire) can be increased.
- The strength of the magnetic field can be increased.

HT The induced voltage depends on the rate at which the magnetic field changes. The rate that the magnetic field changes can be increased by increasing the speed of movement.

AC Generators

The diagram below shows how an AC **generator** works. It is like a motor working in **reverse**.

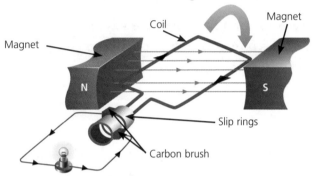

You will need to be able to label a diagram like this one.

HT How AC Generators Work

An AC generator is like a DC motor working in reverse. The difference is that the AC generator has **slip rings** and **brushes** instead of split-ring commutators. The slip rings and brushes are the important parts of the generator because they are what make the generator able to generate alternating current.

The brushes make contact with the slip rings enabling the current to flow while the coil is rotating freely. But the direction of the current changes each half cycle. The side of the coil moving up has current induced in one direction while the side of the coil moving down has current induced in the opposite direction. Once the coil has rotated one half turn, the opposite sides are now moving up and down and so the current flowing in them is now in the opposite direction from before.

This is how an AC generator ensures that the current changes direction every half cycle.

Transformers

A **transformer** can change the size of an alternating voltage – it does not change AC into DC. Transformers need AC to work – they do not work with DC.

① A **transformer** is made of two coils of wire wound onto a common iron core. The two coils of wire are not connected to each other in any way.

② **Step-up** transformers **increase** voltage. They have more coils on the secondary coil than on the primary coil.

② **Step-down** transformers **decrease** voltage. They have fewer coils on the secondary coil than on the primary coil. Step-down transformers are used in phone chargers, laptops and radios.

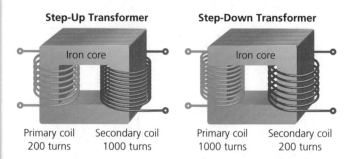

Step-Up Transformer	Step-Down Transformer
Iron core	Iron core
Primary coil 200 turns Secondary coil 1000 turns	Primary coil 1000 turns Secondary coil 200 turns

Transformers and AC

④ Transformers can only use AC because they rely on a changing magnetic field in the primary coil to induce a voltage in the secondary coil. Only alternating current gives the changing magnetic field that the coils need. A direct current will only provide a steady magnetic field and this will not induce a voltage in the secondary coil.

⑤ As the AC increases in the primary coil, the magnetic field it produces grows and cuts through the wire of the secondary coil and induces a current (to try to cancel out the magnetic field from the primary coil).

As the AC in the primary coil falls, the current in the secondary coil is induced in the opposite direction to try to support the magnetic field.

Calculations on Transformers

The voltage on the secondary coil can be calculated from the voltage on the primary coil (and vice versa) using the formula:

⑥ $$\frac{V_p}{V_s} = \frac{N_p}{N_s}$$

V_p = voltage on primary coil
V_s = voltage on secondary coil
N_p = number of turns on primary coil
N_s = number of turns on secondary coil

Example

A laptop computer runs on 12V so if it is to be plugged into the mains (230V), a transformer is needed. If the transformer has 960 turns on the primary coil, how many does it have on the secondary coil?

$$\frac{V_p}{V_s} = \frac{N_p}{N_s}$$

$$N_s = \frac{(N_p \times V_s)}{V_p} = \frac{(960 \times 12)}{230} = 50$$

The current or voltage in a highly efficient transformer can be calculated using the formula:

$$V_p I_p = V_s I_s$$

V_p = voltage in primary coil
I_p = current in primary coil
V_s = voltage in secondary coil
I_s = current in secondary coil

Example

If a current of 0.3 amps is supplied to a transformer in a laptop computer at a voltage of 230 volts, what current is fed to the laptop after the voltage has been stepped down to 12 volts?

$$V_p I_p = V_s I_s$$

$$230 \times 0.3 = 12 \times I_p$$

$$I_p = \frac{(230 \times 0.3)}{12} = 5.75 \text{ amps}$$

Transformers in the National Grid

When **transmission lines** (power cables) carry current, they get hot. The power loss can be reduced by reducing the current, which means less energy is wasted. Therefore, step-up transformers are used to increase the voltage from power stations to supply the **National Grid**. Step-down transformers are used in substations to reduce the voltage for domestic and commercial users.

> **HT**
>
> The power loss in transmission depends on the current squared, therefore if the current is halved, the power loss is only one quarter of what it was originally. The current can be reduced by increasing the voltage using a step-up transformer.
>
> $P = I^2R$
>
> The transformer equation (see page 98) shows that the power input to a transformer is equal to the power output of the transformer. In a step-up transformer, the voltage is increased, but the current is decreased in the same proportion. Because a lower current will reduce power loss during transmission, using a step-up transformer at the power station to increase the voltage has the effect of reducing the energy lost as the current flows along the power cables.
>
> A step-down transformer reduces the voltage to a safer level for consumers (but increases the current).

③ Isolating Transformers

An **isolating transformer** is used in some mains circuits, for example, a bathroom shaver socket, to make them safer.

The two coils in an isolating transformer are not connected to each other in any way, which means that the user is isolated from the mains supply. This is particularly important in bathrooms, where water is present. The isolating transformer does not affect the voltage because the two coils have the same number of turns.

An Isolating Transformer

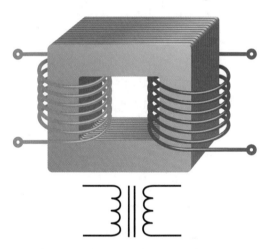

> **HT ⑨ How an Isolating Transformer Works**
>
> An isolating transformer has equal numbers of turns on the primary and secondary coils. This makes no difference to the voltage.
>
> The benefit of an isolating transformer is that it keeps the two halves of the circuit separate. Therefore, there is less risk of contact between the live parts (connected to the mains) and the earth lead (connected to the body of, for example, a hairdryer). This means that the device is safer.

Diodes

A **diode** is a device that allows current to flow through it in one direction only. The symbol for a diode is ─▷|─. The direction of the current is the direction the ▷ points in.

Current–Voltage Curve for a Diode

If the current through a diode is plotted against the voltage across the diode, a **current–voltage characteristic** can be created for the diode:

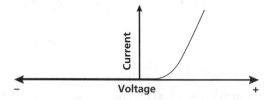

From this graph, it can be seen that the current flows easily through the diode in one direction but not in the opposite direction. The direction of current flow is in the direction of the arrowhead on the symbol.

Half-wave Rectification

If alternating current is passed through a diode, the diode will allow current flowing in one direction to pass through and will stop current flowing in the opposite direction. This is **half-wave rectification**.

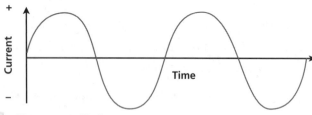

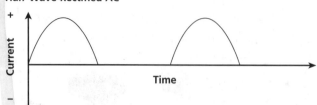

Full-wave Rectification

A group of four diodes can be connected together to make a **bridge rectifier circuit** to give **full-wave rectification**.

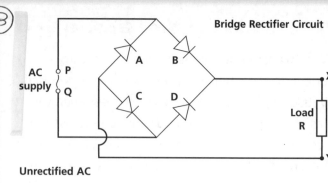

Bridge Rectifier Circuit

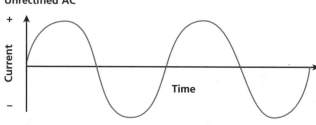

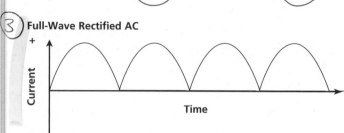

Capacitors

A **capacitor** stores charge that can be discharged later. The symbol for a capacitor is ─||─.

When current flows in a circuit containing an uncharged capacitor, the charge is stored on the capacitor and this makes its pd increase.

When a charged capacitor is connected to a conductor, the capacitor behaves like a **battery** and sends current through the conductor. This makes the capacitor charge reduce, eventually to zero.

When a conductor is connected across a capacitor and current flows through the conductor, the current flow is not constant but dies away as the capacitor's charge decreases.

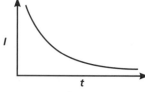

Some devices need a more constant (smooth) voltage supplied to them. A capacitor connected across a voltage supply will produce a more constant (smoothed) output as it discharges slightly to prop up a supply if its own current fails.

HT *I–V* Curves for Diodes

From the current–voltage characteristic curve (on page 100) it is clear that current flows easily in one direction through the diode because it has a low resistance to current in this direction. However, current does not flow easily in the opposite direction because the diode has a high resistance to current flow in the reverse direction.

N.B. The current–voltage characteristic curve for a diode is very different from the curve for an ohmic conductor and for a non-ohmic conductor like a light bulb. Make sure you can remember which is which.

More about Diodes

A silicon diode is made of two types of silicon:
* One contains extra electrons (called **n-type** because of its extra negative charge carriers).
* The other has **holes** where there should be electrons (called **p-type** because holes are like positive charge carriers).

Both types of silicon are uncharged because there are still the same number of electrons and protons in each atom.

When the diode is **forward biased** in a circuit (i.e. the n-type is connected to the negative terminal of the battery), current can flow because the electrons are pushed towards the holes and the holes are pushed towards the electrons. But if the diode is **reverse biased** ('backwards') the current cannot flow because the electrons and holes are pulled apart and are unable to get past the layer between the two types of silicon.

Bridge Circuits

A **bridge circuit** can supply full-wave rectification of AC. For each half of the AC cycle, there is a diode that can pass the current, and send it towards the output. This way, the positive-going half cycle and the negative-going half cycle are both fed to the output as positive half cycles.

Current and Voltage in Discharging Capacitors

If a conductor is connected across a charged capacitor, the charge on the capacitor will flow through the conductor until the capacitor is fully discharged. However, the current does not flow steadily through the conductor. Instead the current decreases as the charge on the capacitor decreases.

As the charge on the capacitor decreases, the pd across the capacitor also decreases. This means that the pd across the conductor has reduced and so the current flowing also reduces. This continues until all the charge has been removed from the capacitor. This gives the graph shown on page 100 for how the current decreases as the capacitor discharges.

Simple Smoothing

In the circuit below, a capacitor **smoothes** the output by discharging when the pd falls to a certain level, thus boosting the current and making sure it remains constant.

When the pd in the circuit is high enough, the capacitor charges up again and remains charged until the pd falls and the capacitor has to make up the difference. This is how it ensures that the output remains constant.

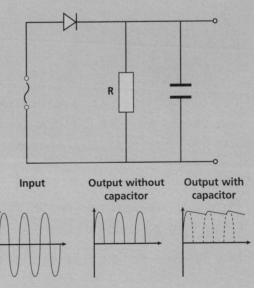

| Input | Output without capacitor | Output with capacitor |

1 Name each of these symbols. [6]

a) b) c) d) e) f)

2 This is a graph of current against voltage for two ohmic conductors.

a) What can you say about the relationship between current and voltage? [1]

b) What does the gradient of the graph represent? [1]

c) Looking at the graph, what can you say about the difference in resistance between the two ohmic conductors, and how do you know? [2]

3 Transformers are found in many everyday appliances such as phone chargers and laptop computers.

a) What do transformers in these appliances do? Tick (✓) the correct answer. [1]

Change AC to DC ☐   Decrease the voltage ☐

Increase the voltage ☐   Change DC to AC ☐

b) Draw a step-up transformer. [2]

c) Sometimes an isolating transformer is used. Explain when it would be used and why. [2]

HT 4 A wire with current running through it has a magnetic field associated with it.

a) Draw the magnetic field on the diagram, including the direction of the field. [1]

b) If the current-carrying wire is put in a magnetic field, the wire will move. Draw arrows on the diagram to show which way the coil of wire would move. [1]

c) This induced movement can be used to create a DC motor.
Explain how you could increase the speed of a motor. [3]

d) How is the direction of the force on the coil in a DC motor maintained? [2]

P1: Energy for the Home

1. a) The ice lolly is melting.
   b) $0.057kg \times 1.34kJ/kg/°C \times 5°C = 0.382kJ$
2. a) 30 years; 1.5 years; 20 years
   b) **Accept any suitable suggestion with reasons, e.g.** Double glazing because it has the biggest annual saving; Draught excluders because they have the shortest payback time / lowest cost.
   c) Foil reflects **[1 mark]** heat energy (infrared) **[1 mark]** back into the room / less heat loss so radiators can be turned down. **[1 mark]**
3. a) Microwave signals
   b) Speed = frequency × wavelength
      $$Frequency = \frac{3 \times 10^8}{0.02}$$
      $$= 1.5 \times 10^{10}\,Hz$$ **[1 mark for calculation, 1 mark for correct answer]**
   c) The town is next to a hill **[1 mark]** Microwaves are transmitted between transmitters and receivers in line of sight and the hill acts as an obstacle. **[1 mark]**
   d) **Advantage:** Improved mobile phone signal for residents. **[1 mark]**
      Disadvantage: The mast could damage the visual appearance of the area; There are concerns that it could be a danger to health. **[Any one for 1 mark]**

P2: Living for the Future (Energy Resources)

1. a) The coil rotates/moves near to the magnet **[1 mark]** which induces (generates) an electric current in the wire. **[1 mark]**
   b) $\frac{Energy\ out}{Energy\ in} \times 100\%$
      $\left(\frac{25}{100}\right) \times 100\% = 25\%$ **[1 mark for calculation, 1 mark for correct answer]**
2. a) Beta radiation **and** Gamma waves. **[1 mark each]**.
   b) Wear protective clothing; Use tongs/keep your distance; Short exposure time; Shielded and labelled storage. **[Any two for 2 marks]**.

3. **This is a model answer, which demonstrates QWC, and would score the full 6 marks:**
   The Ptolemaic and Copernican models are similar in that they both proposed that the planets were represented by glass spheres a fixed distance from the Sun, and that the stars were in fixed positions on the outermost sphere.
   The two models are different in that the Copernican model stated that the Sun was at the centre of the Universe, the Earth rotates once every 24 hours and the Earth takes one full year to revolve around the Sun. In contrast, the Ptolemaic model stated that the Earth was the centre of the Universe.
4. a) Short wavelength electromagnetic radiation from the Sun is absorbed by and heats the Earth **[1 mark]**; The Earth radiates the heat as longer wavelength infrared radiation **[1 mark]**; Greenhouse gases absorb some infrared radiation, which is re-emitted back to Earth, warming the atmosphere. **[1 mark]**
   b) Dust **[1 mark]** released into the atmosphere from the factory would cause radiation from a nearby town to be reflected back to the Earth, causing warming. **[1 mark]**
   c) Visual pollution; Dependent on wind speed; Appropriate space and position needed. **[Any two for 2 marks]**
   d) **This is a model answer, which demonstrates QWC and would score the full 6 marks:** There has been a measured increase in the global temperature and an increase in the level of greenhouse gases such as carbon dioxide and methane in the atmosphere, which leads some to conclude that the greenhouse gases are causing the global temperature increase. Others indicate that global temperatures have increased (and decreased) on many occasions in the past and that there is evidence that solar activity is responsible. There is no doubt that global temperatures are rising but the disagreement is whether greenhouse gases are the cause.

Answers

P3: Forces for Transport

1. a) i) A to B – He is travelling at a steady speed away from home
    ii) B to C – He is stationary
    iii) C to D – He is travelling at a steady speed towards home

b) Faster on the way there than on the way back (steeper slope).

c) Away from home $= \dfrac{300}{50} = 6\,\text{m/s}$ **[1 mark]**

Towards home $= \dfrac{300}{100} = 3\,\text{m/s}$ **[1 mark]**

d)

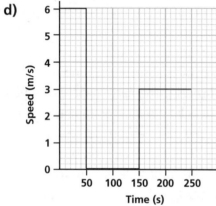

[2 marks for correct lines, 1 mark for correct labelling of axes]

2. a) $35 + 45 = 80\,\text{m}$

b) **Thinking distance:** The speed of the car **[1 mark]**; The reaction time of the driver e.g. the driver has been drinking alcohol. **[1 mark]**
Braking distance: The weight of the car; The speed of the car; The road conditions. **[Any two for 2 marks]**.

c) Absorb energy during a crash by crumpling up **[1 mark]**; This dissipates the energy more slowly, reducing the momentum of the crash **[1 mark]**; Reducing injuries to the passengers. **[1 mark]**

3. a) change in momentum $= m_1v_1 - m_2v_2 = (1300 \times 22.3) - (1300 \times 13.4) = 28990 - 17420 = 11570\,\text{kgm/s}$ **[1 mark for calculation, 1 mark for correct answer]**

b) i) change in momentum $= m_1v_1 - m_2v_2 = (1300 \times 13.4) - (1300 \times 0) = 17420 - 0 = 17420\,\text{kgm/s}$ **[1 mark for calculation, 1 mark for correct answer]**

ii) Force = change in momentum ÷ time $= 17420 \div 2.2 = 7918.2\,\text{N}$ **[2 marks for calculation, 1 mark for correct answer]**

4. a) GPE = mgh
    $= 80 \times 10 \times 30$
    $= 24000\,\text{J}$ **[1 mark for calculation, 1 mark for correct answer]**

b) KE = GPE
KE = 24000
$24000 = \tfrac{1}{2}mv^2$
$v = 24.4948....$
$v = 24.5\,\text{m/s}$
[1 mark for calculation, 1 mark for correct answer]

c) Acceleration $= \dfrac{\text{change in speed}}{\text{time}}$
$= \dfrac{-24.5}{2} = -12.25\,\text{m/s}^2$
[1 mark for calculation, 1 mark for correct answer]

P4: Radiation for Life

1. a) Brown – Live
Green/yellow – Earth
Blue – Neutral

b) If the current becomes too large the fuse melts **[1 mark]**, breaking the circuit. **[1 mark]**

c) No **[1 mark]**; They do not need earthing because the case is a non-conductor and cannot become live. **[1 mark]**

2. a) It decreases.

b) A helium nucleus or two protons + two neutrons.

c) In a smoke detector **[1 mark]**; Smoke particles hit by alpha particles; Less ionisation of air particles, causing the current to be reduced and the alarm to sound. **[Any one for 1 mark]**

3. a) Rubbing the two insulating materials together allows electrons to transfer between objects. **[1 mark]**
The duster becomes positively charged due to lack of electrons and the balloon becomes negatively charged due to an excess of electrons. **[1 mark]**

Answers

b) The balloon repels the electrons on the atoms on the surface of the wall; **[1 mark]** This gives the wall a slight positive charge at the surface and the balloon is then attracted to the wall as opposite charges attract. **[1 mark]**

c) Using shoes with insulating soles; **[1 mark]** Not touching the metal parts of the car until the charge on his body has leaked away. **[1 mark]**

P5: Space for Reflection

1. a) $W = m \times g$
$= 70 \times 2$
$= 140N$ **[1 mark for calculation, 1 mark for correct answer]**

b) Gravity is the universal force of attraction between masses.

c) An object that orbits a larger object in space.

d) Communications; Weather forecasting; Military uses; Scientific research; GPS. **[Any two for 2 marks]**

2. a) It is being refracted.

b) The waves travel from one medium to another **[1 mark]**; This causes the wave speed to change and the wave to change direction. **[1 mark]**

c) Refractive index = $\dfrac{\text{speed of light in vacuum}}{\text{speed of light in medium}}$

Refractive index = $\dfrac{3 \times 10^8}{2 \times 10^8} = \dfrac{3}{2}$

Refractive index = 1.5 **[1 mark for calculation, 1 mark for correct answer]**

3. a) Mass: Scalar **[1 mark]**; Force: Vector **[1 mark]**; Velocity: Vector **[1 mark]**; Time: Scalar **[1 mark]**; Acceleration: Vector **[1 mark]**

b) $s = \left(\dfrac{(u + v)}{2}\right) \times t$
$= 2 \times 3$ **[1 mark]** $= 6m$ **[1 mark]**

c) Either: $a = \dfrac{(v^2 - u^2)}{2s}$
$a = 1.33333$ **[1 mark]**
$= 1.3m/s^2$ **[1 mark]**

Or: $a = \dfrac{(s - ut)^2}{t^2}$
$= 1.3333$ **[1 mark]**
$= 1.3m/s^2$ **[1 mark]**

P6: Electricity for Gadgets

1. a) Resistor; **b)** Bulb; **c)** Cell; **d)** Switch; **e)** Variable resistor; **f)** Power supply.

2. a) As current increases, voltage increases.

b) Resistance

c) Ohmic conductor B has a greater resistance **[1 mark]**; It has a steeper gradient **[1 mark]**

3. a) Decrease the voltage.

b)

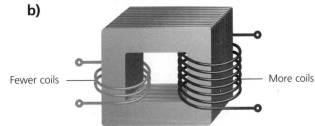

Fewer coils — More coils

[All correct for 2 marks]

c) In a bathroom shaver socket for example **[1 mark]**; For safety reasons when water is around. The user is isolated from the mains supply, making them safer. **[1 mark]**

4. a)

b)

c) Increase the size of the electric current **[1 mark]**; Increase the number of turns on the coil **[1 mark]**; Increase the strength of the magnetic field. **[1 mark]**

d) The current changes direction every half turn **[1 mark]**; Due to there being a split-ring commutator. **[1 mark]**

Glossary

Acceleration – rate of increase of speed (calculated as speed change divided by time taken and measured in m/s²) or change in direction of an object.

Air resistance – the frictional force that acts on a moving object.

Alpha radiation – nuclear radiation particle made up of 2 protons and 2 neutrons.

Alternating current (AC) – an electric current that changes direction of flow repeatedly.

Amplitude – the maximum disturbance of a wave from a central position.

Analogue – signal that varies continuously in amplitude or frequency.

Asteroid – large rock (smaller than a planet) that orbits the Sun in a belt between Mars and Jupiter – occasionally knocked off course by other rocks.

Attraction – the drawing together of materials with different charges.

Background radiation – radiation from soil, rocks and other things in the environment.

Beta radiation – nuclear radiation made up of a fast moving electron.

Big Bang theory – theory of how the Universe started.

Biomass – natural materials such as wood or manure that can be burned or fermented to produce methane as a fuel.

Black hole – formed at the end of a star's life; has very dense core which exerts extreme gravity so that even light cannot escape.

Braking distance – the distance that a car travels during braking to a stop.

Capacitor – an electrical device that accumulates and temporarily stores electrical charge; used for smoothing AC.

Chain reaction – in a nuclear power station the chain reaction allows the nuclear fusion to continue.

Charge – an electron carries a negative charge.

Circuit – a continuous link of conductors that can carry an electric current.

Climate change – changes in climate that result in increasing average global temperatures.

Coherent light waves – light that has the same wavelength or frequency and is in phase, such as laser light.

Comet – orbits the Sun in an elliptical orbit; has frozen gas and dust core.

Conduction – transfer of thermal or electrical energy.

Conductor – material that transfers thermal or electrical energy.

Convex lens – a lens that causes light rays passing through it to meet at a point (converge).

Critical angle – the largest angle of incidence within a medium at which refraction can occur.

Current – the rate of flow of an electrical charge; measured in amperes (A).

DAB (digital audio broadcasting) – transmitting radio signals using digital signals rather than analogue signals.

Deceleration – rate of decrease in speed of an object.

Deforestation – removal of large areas of forest.

Degrees Celsius (°C) – unit of temperature.

Digital – signal that uses binary code (ons and offs such as Morse code).

Diode – an electrical device that allows electric current to flow in one direction only.

Direct current (DC) – an electric current that flows only in one direction.

Discharge – to remove charge.

Dispersion – (of light) the separation of light into different wavelengths, which represent the colours of the rainbow (visible spectrum).

Distance–time graph – a graph showing distance travelled against time taken; the gradient of the line represents speed.

Drag – resistive or frictional force on moving objects.

Dynamo effect – generating electricity by moving a coil of wire near a magnet.

Earthing – connection between the metal casing of a device and the Earth.

Efficiency – useful output energy expressed as a percentage of total input energy.

Electric current – flow of charge through conductors in a circuit.

Electromagnetic waves / spectrum – includes radio waves, visible light and gamma radiation, all of which travel through a vacuum at the speed of light.

Electron – a negatively charged particle that orbits the nucleus of an atom; a charged particle that flows through wires as an electric current.

Energy – measure of ability to do work or of heat transferred; measured in joules (J).

Fleming's left-hand rule – method for predicting which direction a current-carrying wire will move in a magnetic field.

Focal length – a measure of how strongly an optical system focuses or diverges light; distance from lens centre to the point where parallel rays through the lens converge to a point.

Focal point – the point at which all light rays parallel to the axis of the lens converge.

Force – a push or pull acting on an object; measured in newtons (N).

Fossil fuel – coal, oil and natural gas.

Frequency – of AC – the number of cycles completed each second; of waves – the number of waves produced (or that pass a particular point) in one second.

Friction – the resistive force between two surfaces as they move over each other.

Full-wave rectification – using diodes to convert AC to create current flowing in one direction.

Fuse – thin metal wire designed to melt to break a circuit when it is overloaded.

Gamma radiation – nuclear radiation that is high frequency electromagnetic waves.

Geiger counter – a device for measuring radioactivity.

Generator – a device for making electric current using a magnet and a coil of wire.

Generator – a device for making electric current using a magnet and a coil of wire moving relative to each other.

Geostationary satellite – satellite that orbits the Earth above the Equator taking 24 hours for one orbit and therefore staying above the same point on the Earth.

Gravitational potential energy – the energy an object has because of its mass and height above Earth.

Gravity (gravitational force) – a force of attraction between masses.

Greenhouse effect – trapping of heat by the atmosphere.

Incident angle – angle measured from the normal at which light approaches a boundary between two materials.

Infrared – hotter objects emit more infrared radiation than cooler objects. Infrared is a form of electromagnetic radiation.

Insulation – material containing air pockets that reduces heat loss by conduction.

Insulator – a substance that does not transfer thermal or electrical energy very well.

Interference – on a radio the hissing noise is interference as a result of the signal being corrupted; two waves can interfere and either reinforce each other or cancel out.

Ion – a charged particle formed when an atom gains or loses an electron.

Ionising – radiation that turns atoms into ions.

Joule (J) – unit of energy.

Kilowatt hour – a measure of how much electrical energy has been used.

Kinetic energy (KE) – the energy possessed by a body because of its movement.

Light dependent resistor (LDR) – device where the resistance reduces if light falls on it.

Logic gates – devices that take inputs (high or low) in combination and produce specific outputs.

Longitudinal wave – an energy-carrying wave where the particles of the medium move in the direction of energy transfer.

Magnetic field – the area of effect of a magnet (or the Earth) indicated by lines of force surrounding the magnet (or the Earth).

Magnification – the size of an image relative to the object; measured as image height ÷ object height.

Mass – the quantity of matter in an object.

Melt – to change from solid to liquid.

Meteor – small rock orbiting a star.

Microwaves – electromagnetic waves that can be used for transmitting messages and for cooking.

Momentum – a measure of the state of motion of an object; product of its mass and velocity.

Neutron – uncharged particle in the nucleus of an atom.

Neutron star – star made of neutrons.

Nuclear fission – the splitting of atomic nuclei giving out energy.

Nuclear fuel – non-renewable fuel that generates heat from fission reactions e.g. uranium or plutonium.

Nuclear fusion – two atoms joining together giving out energy.

Nuclear power – generating electricity using uranium or plutonium as the fuel to transfer heat.

Nuclear radiation – alpha or beta particles or gamma radiation given off from radioactive materials.

Ohmic resistor – device that follows Ohm's law – its current increases in proportion to the voltage put across it.

Optical fibre – thin glass fibre that carries digital signals.

Orbit – the path of an object around a larger object.

Orbital period – the time it takes an object to make one complete orbit.

Ozone – a gas in the upper atmosphere.

Parabolic – curved trajectory of a projectile.

Payback time – the time taken for insulation to pay for itself from savings made.

Photocell – a device that captures light energy and transforms it into electrical energy.

Plutonium – radioactive fuel used in some nuclear power stations.

Potential divider – device for creating specific voltage output from a (larger voltage) supply.

Power – the rate of doing work; measured in watts (W).

Primary waves (P-waves) – earthquake waves that travel through the Earth arriving at the detector first.

Projectile – object launched and flying through the air.

Radiation – electromagnetic waves or particles emitted by a radioactive substance; transfer of heat as infrared electromagnetic radiation.

Radio waves – long wavelength electromagnetic waves.

Radioactive – substance that emits radiation.

Real image – an image produced by rays of light meeting at a point; can be projected onto a screen.

Red giant – in their life cycle some stars will explode to form a red giant.

Reflection – change in direction of a wave back into a medium at a boundary between two media.

Refraction – change in direction of a wave as it passes from one medium to another and changes speed.

Refractive index – measure of a medium's ability to bend light due to slowing the light down.

Reinforcement – two beams of light can interfere with and reinforce each other resulting in a higher intensity light.

Relative speed – the speed of an object, relative to another object that is treated as being at rest.

Relay – an electrical device that uses a small current in one circuit to make or break a connection to switch another circuit where a larger current flows.

Renewable – energy sources that will not run out.

Repulsion – the pushing away of materials that have the same charge.

Resistance – how hard it is to get a current through a component at a particular potential difference; measured in ohms (Ω).

Rheostat – variable resistor used to control electric current.

Satellite – an object that orbits a planet, e.g. the Moon

Scalar quantity – a quantity where only the size is important, e.g. mass.

Secondary waves (S-waves) – earthquake waves that travel through the Earth and arrive second at the detector.

Seismic wave – wave produced by an earthquake.

Seismometer – machine used to detect seismic waves.

Glossary

Specific heat capacity – value of how much energy a material requires, per kilogram, to raise its temperature by 1°C.

Specific latent heat – heat energy required to melt or boil 1kg of a material.

Speed – the rate at which an object moves in m/s – a scalar quantity.

Speed–time graph – a graph showing speed against time; the gradient of the line represents acceleration; the area under the line represents distance.

State (of matter) – whether a material is solid, liquid or gas.

Static electricity – electricity that is produced by friction and does not flow.

Step-down transformer – device that reduces the AC voltage fed to it (and increases the current).

Step-up transformer – device that increases the AC voltage fed to it (and reduces the current).

Stopping distance – calculated as thinking distance + braking distance.

Supernova – an exploding star.

Temperature – the degree of hotness of an object measured in degrees Celsius (°C).

Thermistor – device in which the resistance reduces when it becomes warm.

Thermogram – image showing the different temperatures of an object through different colours.

Thinking distance – distance that a car travels while the driver reacts and starts to brake.

Total internal reflection – complete reflection of a light or infrared ray back into a medium.

Total internal reflection – complete reflection of a light or infrared ray back into a medium.

Tracer – a radioactive substance that can be followed and detected.

Trajectory – the path followed by a projectile (moving body).

Transfer – move energy from one place to another.

Transform – change energy from one form to another, e.g. kinetic to electrical.

Transformer – an electrical device that changes the voltage of alternating currents.

Transistor – electronic device that acts as a switch to a larger circuit when a small current is fed in.

Transverse wave – a wave in which the vibrations are at 90° to the direction of energy transfer.

Truth table – shows the output of a group of logic gates.

Ultrasound – sound waves with a frequency above 20 000Hz.

Uranium – radioactive material used as fuel in a nuclear power station.

Variable resistor – rheostat; resistor whose resistance can be varied.

Vector quantity – a quantity where both size and direction are important, e.g. acceleration, force.

Velocity – an object's rate of displacement (change of distance) in a particular direction; a measure of displacement divided by time – a vector quantity.

Voltage (potential difference) – the difference in potential between two points in an electrical circuit; the energy transferred in a circuit by each coulomb of charge; measured in volts (V).

Watt – unit of power.

Wavelength – the distance between corresponding points on two adjacent disturbances.

Weight – the force of an object on the Earth due to gravity pulling the object towards the centre of the Earth.

White dwarf – in the life cycle of a star, a medium-sized star will collapse to form a white dwarf.

Work – energy used moving a force through a distance; measured in joules(J).

HT

Centripetal force – the external force towards the centre of a circle required to make an object follow a circular path at a constant speed.

Convection – transfer of heat energy involving the movement of the substance.

Diffraction – the spreading out of a wave as a result of passing an obstacle or passing through a gap.

Fleming's left-hand rule – method for predicting which direction a current-carrying wire will move in a magnetic field.

Half-life – the time taken for half the atoms in radioactive material to decay.

Half-wave rectification – either the positive or negative half of an AC wave is allowed to pass through a diode, while the other half is blocked.

Ionosphere – band of charged particles (ions) in the Earth's atmosphere.

Light year – measure of distance; travelled by light in a year.

Monochromatic – monochromatic light has a single wavelength.

Multiplex – sending more than one signal along an optical fibre at a time, using different wavelengths.

Path difference – difference in distance travelled by two beams of light before interfering.

Phase – two waves are in phase if they have peaks and troughs occurring together.

Polarisation – the blocking of light waves that oscillate in certain directions, for example, how sunglasses cut out glare.

Slip ring – in an AC generator this allows the coil to turn as current is generated.

Smoothing – using a capacitor to make an AC supply more constant.

Split-ring commutator – in a DC generator this allows the current to flow the same way at all times to maintain rotation.

Terminal speed – a steady falling speed, when the weight of an object is equal and opposite to its air resistance.

Virtual image – an image produced by rays of light appearing to come from a point; cannot be projected onto a screen; image seen through magnifying glass.

Periodic Table

Key

| relative atomic mass |
| **atomic symbol** |
| name |
| atomic (proton) number |

1	2											3	4	5	6	7	0
																	4 **He** helium 2
7 **Li** lithium 3	9 **Be** beryllium 4											11 **B** boron 5	12 **C** carbon 6	14 **N** nitrogen 7	16 **O** oxygen 8	19 **F** fluorine 9	20 **Ne** neon 10
23 **Na** sodium 11	24 **Mg** magnesium 12											27 **Al** aluminium 13	28 **Si** silicon 14	31 **P** phosphorus 15	32 **S** sulfur 16	35.5 **Cl** chlorine 17	40 **Ar** argon 18
39 **K** potassium 19	40 **Ca** calcium 20	45 **Sc** scandium 21	48 **Ti** titanium 22	51 **V** vanadium 23	52 **Cr** chromium 24	55 **Mn** manganese 25	56 **Fe** iron 26	59 **Co** cobalt 27	59 **Ni** nickel 28	63.5 **Cu** copper 29	65 **Zn** zinc 30	70 **Ga** gallium 31	73 **Ge** germanium 32	75 **As** arsenic 33	79 **Se** selenium 34	80 **Br** bromine 35	84 **Kr** krypton 36
85 **Rb** rubidium 37	88 **Sr** strontium 38	89 **Y** yttrium 39	91 **Zr** zirconium 40	93 **Nb** niobium 41	96 **Mo** molybdenum 42	[98] **Tc** technetium 43	101 **Ru** ruthenium 44	103 **Rh** rhodium 45	106 **Pd** palladium 46	108 **Ag** silver 47	112 **Cd** cadmium 48	115 **In** indium 49	119 **Sn** tin 50	122 **Sb** antimony 51	128 **Te** tellurium 52	127 **I** iodine 53	131 **Xe** xenon 54
133 **Cs** caesium 55	137 **Ba** barium 56	139 **La*** lanthanum 57	178 **Hf** hafnium 72	181 **Ta** tantalum 73	184 **W** tungsten 74	186 **Re** rhenium 75	190 **Os** osmium 76	192 **Ir** iridium 77	195 **Pt** platinum 78	197 **Au** gold 79	201 **Hg** mercury 80	204 **Tl** thallium 81	207 **Pb** lead 82	209 **Bi** bismuth 83	[209] **Po** polonium 84	[210] **At** astatine 85	[222] **Rn** radon 86
[223] **Fr** francium 87	[226] **Ra** radium 88	[227] **Ac*** actinium 89	[261] **Rf** rutherfordium 104	[262] **Db** dubnium 105	[266] **Sg** seaborgium 106	[264] **Bh** bohrium 107	[277] **Hs** hassium 108	[268] **Mt** meitnerium 109	[271] **Ds** darmstadtium 110	[272] **Rg** roentgenium 111							

1
H
hydrogen
1

Elements with atomic numbers 112–116 have been reported but not fully authenticated

*The lanthanoids (atomic numbers 58–71) and the actinoids (atomic numbers 90–103) have been omitted.

Index